PRACTICAL GREEK MAGIC

A complete manual of Olympian Greek magic for those wishing to tread the Heroic Path.

By the same author
PRACTICAL EGYPTIAN MAGIC
PRACTICAL TECHNIQUES OF PSYCHIC SELF-DEFENCE

PRACTICAL GREEK MAGIC

A complete manual of a unique magical system based on the classical legends of ancient Greece.

MURRY HOPE

Illustrated by Martin Jones

THE AQUARIAN PRESS
Wellingborough, Northamptonshire

First published 1985

10 9 8 7 6 5 4 3 2

British Library Cataloguing in Publication Data

Hope, Murry
Practical Greek magic.
1. Occult sciences
I. Title
133 BF1411

ISBN 0-85030-430-X

The Aquarian Press is part of the Thorsons Publishing Group

Printed and bound in Great Britain

'What we are to our inward vision, and what man appears to be *sub speciae aeternitatis*, can only be expressed by way of myth. Myth is more individual and expresses life more precisely than does science.'

Carl Gustav Jung

To Jed

with a Heroine's
love and gratitude.

CONTENTS

INTRODUCTION

Magic is concerned with the conversion of universal energies into practical frequencies that can be utilized according to the needs of the occasion. These energies in themselves are totally neutral, having no affiliation with any belief, system or personality either here on Earth or anywhere in the cosmos, their manifestation at the magical level being coloured entirely by the nature and intention of the user.

Although over the centuries man has devised many methods of effecting this process, the realization will inevitably dawn on him that what he is basically trying to master is the power of his own mind. Mind over matter is by no means as esoteric as many occultists and mystics would have us believe. Because of recent forward strides in holistic healing the concept of self-programming, for example, is slowly acquiring credence among the more stalwart bastions of medical orthodoxy. This does not imply, of course, that it is an easy and trouble-free discipline for, like everything else in life, it needs to be properly learned, digested and understood before it becomes safely practical.

As a study and serious practice, however, it can be approached in many ways and at many levels, some of which have been classified over the centuries into what are termed occult schools, systems or traditions. These schools carry the influence of the culture in which they first flourished and of the individual group or faith that gave birth to them and fostered their infancy. Some of the older traditions such as the Egyptian, Indian and Chaldean have naturally altered considerably over the centuries as successive magi, teachers and reformers have left their mark. But the essence still remains to be rediscovered by the ardent seeker.

Magic and philosophy formed a very real part of early Greek life in that the basic religion contained more than a sprinkling of occult overtones. Like the earlier Egyptian magical system, the Greek school sprang from several sources, some clearly primitive and others superimposed by incoming cultural tides. As time progressed the old religions gave way to the popular mystery cults, the best known of which are probably the Orphic, Dionysiac and Eleusinian, but there is far more to be revealed, as we shall see.

The Greek magical quest is symbolized by the cult of the hero or mortal who, in pursuit of his divinity, is subjected to a series of personal initiations which take the form of mythological deeds. These challenges appear in practical and oft-times very earthly form, in spite of a generous smattering of fabulous beasts and accompanying elemental phenomena, plus some timely help from Olympus. But from an occult standpoint they are purely allegorical and simply represent the trials of the aspiring human soul whose quest takes him into the universe beyond the dimensions of earthly life and experience, where he may eventually be reunited with his source.

The Greeks were nothing if not logical; they employed imaginative and psychologically interesting terms of reference to describe the mental journeys undertaken by those heroic initiates who set forth from their terrestrial origins to conquer the path to Mount Olympus, thus gaining their right of entry into the company of the gods.

The Greek or Heroic Path is the way of the individual albeit with a little assistance from an 'inner planes' tutor and one or maybe more tutelary deities. But it does not call for group effort and, although many occultists of Greek inclination may choose to worship in temple form, ultimately the aspiring Hero stands alone and must face and cope with the oncoming tide of monsters, gremlins and treacherous humans, in addition to his own mental weaknesses and spiritual shortcomings, if he is to attain to his spiritual goal.

A formidable task, perhaps, but in accordance with the

Law of Equalities the weaponry available to the aspiring Hero is equally powerful. So, as long as due respect is paid to the tutelary deities (or, in more general occult terms, cosmic laws are observed) and appreciation shown for their bounty, the aspiring Hero will overcome his mortal dependence, master his ego and receive his well-earned accolades. Should he fail — either himself or those 'powers' whose favours he has elected to receive — the price or penalty could be heavy. As James Dupont (1606–1679) observed: 'Quem Juppiter vult perdere dementat prius.' (Whom the god[s] destroy he[they] first drive mad). Of course, it is not in reality the 'god(s)' who cause the insanity but the man's misuse or rejection of the god aspects within himself that can bring about a mental imbalance varying in degree according to the nature and misdirection of these energies. So, while the lone path may appear easier in that one has only oneself to please, the burden of individual responsibility is a correspondingly greater one.

But it is a path that can be conquered; the answers to the riddles and directions for victory are clearly written within the philosophy of Greek magic, as we shall see.

PART ONE
THE THEORY

1. THE MYTHOLOGICAL HISTORY AND ORIGINS OF THE GREEK MAGICAL SYSTEM

In order to uncover the roots of what can be broadly classified as Greek magic, it is necessary to examine the esoteric/religious heritage and cultural backcloth against which it developed, while also considering the early Greek mystical and magical consciousness in the light of the particular brand of logic so strongly associated with that ethos.

Robert Graves, in his book *The Greek Myths*, is of the opinion that any study involving Greek mythology, or allied credos, should begin with a consideration of the political and religious systems existing in Europe prior to the arrival of the Aryan invaders from the distant north and east. The whole of Neolithic Europe, he tells us, had a remarkably homogeneous system of religious ideas based on the worship of the many-titled mother goddess, who was also known and accepted in Libya and Syria. Ancient Europe did not appear to have gods, only a goddess, the concept of fatherhood not, at that period, having found its way into religious thought. The great goddess took lovers, but for pleasure rather than to father children for her. She was associated with the Moon and, as such, appeared in triple form as maiden, nymph and crone, latterly typified by Artemis, Aphrodite and Hecate. At one period each form was depicted as three persons, making nine in all; but in reality these were all facets of the one great mother or universal goddess.

Graves explains, 'Time was first reckoned by lunations, and every important ceremony took place at a certain phase of the Moon; the solstices and equinoxes not being exactly determined, but approximated to the nearest new or full Moon. The number seven acquired peculiar sanctity, because the king died at the seventh full Moon after the shortest day.' Later, when it was thought that the solar year had only 364 days, plus a few hours (Graves, p.15), it was divided into months — lunar cycles — rather than fractions of the solar cycle. These months, Graves tells us, were known as 'common law months', each being twenty-eight days, as associated with the menstrual cycle in women and the true period of the Moon's revolutions in terms of the Sun. The seven-day week was a unit of the common law month, the character of each being deduced, it seems, from the quality attributed to the corresponding month of the king's life. Thirteen-month years survived among European peasants for more than a millennium after the adoption of the Julian calendar; thirteen, the number of the Sun's death-month, has never lost its evil reputation amongst those who have the old religion deeply embedded in their subconscious or psyche.

According to the Larousse *Encyclopedia of Mythology*, well before the people whom we now know as Greeks had emerged from primitive barbarism, a small pocket of civilization which had already started to flower in the third millennium existed in the basin of the Aegean Sea; it reached its apogee towards the sixth century BC when it spread to continental Greece, starting in Argolis (Mycenae). It was subsequently destroyed in the twelfth century by Dorian invasions.

In this Aegean civilization religion certainly had its place, but we are told that there is insufficient archaeological evidence to allow an exact estimate of its character and elements. Fetishism, it would appear, was much the order of the day, the worship of sacred stones, pillars, weapons, trees and animals being predominant. Later, when an anthropomorphic conception of divinity arose, the Cretan pantheon was formed and the myths were born.

The Aegeans followed the religious pattern favoured by the surrounding countries and cultures of the time, their main deity appearing in feminine form as a great goddess or universal mother. In addition to embodying all the attributes and functions that modern religions bestow upon their patriarchal god, she also symbolized fertility and her influence was by no means limited to the sphere of human experience and consciousness. She cared equally for animals, plants, minerals and all living things. The whole universe was her domain, which meant that she was mistress of heavenly or extra-terrestrial activities, as well as all orders of life upon the planet Earth.

This 'great goddess' appeared in many forms, sometimes crouching, sometimes standing, often nude; but the best and most famous representation shows her in a dress with a flounced skirt and a corsage that left the breasts exposed in true Cretan style. The headgear varied from a highly decorated turban or tiara to free-flowing locks.

Doubtless there were numerous variations of the goddess theme from place to place, according to the nature and inclinations of the indigenous populations. Sometimes she appeared as a vegetation deity or as a sea goddess conveyed across the waves in a magical boat; at other times she was envisaged as a warrior lady escorted by a lion, or as the Earth goddess around whom the serpents of wisdom and knowledge entwined. Her name we do not know for sure, but classical conjecture has it that she was probably Rhea. Zeus was sometimes referred to as her son, a tradition revived by Hesiod in his *Theogony*.

Two other names by which she is sometimes known are Dictynna and Britomartis. Dictynna, whom the Greeks called 'the goddess of the nets', was no doubt connected with Mount Dicte, a mountain in Crete that was later said to be the birthplace of Zeus. This would therefore be her 'mother goddess' role; while as Britomartis, 'the sweet virgin', she assumed the maiden archetype in much the same mode as Artemis, the virgin huntress.

The Aegean great goddess did have a mate, however, and the name Asterius (the starry) has come down to us. He re-emerges later under the name Asterion, king of Crete, who married Europa after her adventure with Zeus and from then onwards appeared to have assimilated the attributes of the sky god himself. The Cretan god can be identified by the mingling of the animal and the human features of which his nature appears to have been composed. The bull was adopted by the Aegeans as a symbol of strength and creative energy and became an important feature in Cretan legends and beliefs. In his animal form the bull god was the Minotaur and as a human he was Minos. Later Hellenization induced considerable modifications in all the earlier Aegean beliefs and legends and they do not reappear until the heroic legends of classical Greece, when they (and other earlier phenomena) serve as bizarre encounters, testing grounds and enemies or allies of the heroes of old.

The Greek pantheon can be dated back to the Homeric epoch. The numerous divinities of which it was composed appear in the *Iliad* and the *Odyssey* with their typical characteristics and personal nature and legends, but the poet tells us nothing of their origins. Zeus is mentioned as being the son of Cronus, while Oceanus and his spouse Tethys were said to have spawned both gods and mortals. We are back to our emergence from the sea theme, rather after the style of the earlier Egyptian depictions (British Museum) which show the birthplace of the gods as some watery Eden to the west.

Later in their history the Greeks thought it proper to provide their gods with a genealogy and a history. Hesiod's *Theogony*, written *circa* the eighth century BC, is the oldest Greek attempt at mythological classification; it presented a cosmogony, as much as a theogony, that was officially recognized as worthy of some status or general acceptance within the communities of the time.

From the sixth century BC, however, until the beginning of the Christian era, other theogonies, which departed widely from the Hesiodic traditions, emerged under the influence of Orphism. But the Orphic mysteries were known only to the initiated and were therefore not normally available to the general populace. They were also rather too strongly Asiatically flavoured to be specifically Greek in character.

In order to discover and analyse those occult traditions that contributed to what may be broadly termed 'Greek magic' a consideration of the early creation myths is essential, as these do throw some considerable light on our quest, with Robert Graves again as our major source of reference.

The Pelasgian Creation Myth

In the beginning Eurynome, the goddess of all things, rose naked from chaos but finding nothing substantial for her feet to rest upon she divided the sea from the sky, set the winds in motion and commenced the work of creation. The great serpent Ophion was her first effort and after coupling with him she assumed the form of a dove and laid the universal egg. At her bidding Ophion coiled seven times about this egg until it hatched and split in two. Out tumbled all that exists, her children, the Sun, Moon, planets, stars and Earth as we see and know it. Eurynome and Ophion made their home on Mount Olympus, but he upset her by claiming that *he* had created the universe, so she bruised his head with her heel, kicked out his teeth and banished him to the dark caves below the Earth.

In addition to the Biblical reverberances, this tale presents us with some highly interesting metaphysical data. Eurynome emerges as yet another prototype of the Virgin Mary, the latter frequently being depicted crushing the head of the serpent beneath her feet; while the Ophion/Lucifer inference is blatantly obvious. It is interesting to compare this version with the Egyptian legend where Ra, the Sun god, assumes the Eurynome role, while his old enemy Typhon is put to flight by his daughter, the cat goddess Bast; a good example of how the archetype can manifest as either sex according to currently fashionable trends in religious or philosophical thought.

To return to our goddess. Next, we are told, she 'created the seven planetary powers, setting a Titaness and a Titan over each. Theia and Hyperion for the Sun; Phoebe and Atlas for the Moon; Dione and Crius for the planet Mars; Metis and Coeus for the planet Mercury; Themis and Eurymedon for the planet Jupiter; Tethys and Oceanus for Venus; Rhea and Cronus for the planet Saturn. But the first man was Pelasgus, ancestor of the Pelasgians; he sprang from the soil of Arcadia, followed by certain others, whom he taught to make huts and feed upon acorns, and sew pigskin tunics such as poor folk still wear in Euboea and Phocis.' (Graves, p.27). So it would appear that at some point the Pelasgians came into contact with a sophisticated theogony that influenced both their culture and lifestyle. Their kinship with the pre-Olympian goddess cult is also obvious.

The Homeric and Orphic Creation Myths

According to Orphic tradition, black-winged Night, a goddess whom even the major gods held in awe, was courted by the Wind and laid a silver egg in the womb of Darkness. From this egg Eros emerged to set the universe in motion. Eros was double-sexed, golden-winged, had four heads and sometimes roared like a bull or lion, hissed like a serpent, or bleated like a ram. Night named him both Ericepaius and Protegenus Phaëton and dwelt with him in a cave. She displayed herself as a triad: Night, Order and Justice. Before this cave sat the mother goddess Rhea playing on a brazen drum to compel man's attention to her oracles. Eros (also called Phanes) created Earth, Sky, Sun and Moon, but the triple goddess ruled the universe and her sceptre passed to Uranus.

The Orphic cult itself will be dealt with in a later chapter, but there are a few details worthy of comment at this point, notably the 'cosmic egg' theme which constantly recurs in these myths. Certain psychics in our present day and age, who claim to be in contact with civilizations from other parts of the universe, have been given information concerning the breeding habits of a particular race which was supposedly responsible for the 'seeding' of Earth. These people apparently reproduced themselves through an external ova system, the fertilized seed growing in egg form outside the womb and not through an extended period of internal gestation such as we experience here.

Another interesting point concerns the nature of Eros himself. The love principle is often bandied about on our planet as either a reproductive convenience or a source of carnal pleasure; esoterically, its higher octaves are involved with a purer and truer set of cosmic values as taught by the great teachers and enlightened ones down the ages. The Eros figure of Orphic myth is dually sexed; its *anima* and *animus* are perfectly balanced and its four heads signify the fully realized fourfold nature of a spiritually ascended being, the elemental qualities having been met and mastered. Much of this teaching would appear to have crept into Gnostic Christianity, leaving its mark, for example, on the four evangelists and the golden-winged seraphim. The triple goddess story obviously relates to pre-Aryan goddess cults, the influence of which still prevails in modern Wicca and among those who have striven to re-establish the older pre-Christian faiths in a profound effort to discover their real spiritual roots.

So far, three distinct influences emerge from this enquiry: the obvious and well-documented matriarchal tradition; the more violent patriarchal deities or the conquerors who took over the reins by force; and a deeper and more significant strain that echoed profoundly throughout the pantheons of those early periods. The latter represents the magical or esoteric teachings of an older and spiritually advanced people whom we may designate Sumerians, Mu'ans, Atlanteans, or extra-terrestrials, according to our faith or inclination.

The Olympian Creation Myth

According to Hesiod, in the beginning was Chaos, vast and dark. Then appeared Gaea, the deep-breasted Earth; and finally Eros, the 'love that softens hearts'. From Chaos were born Erebus and Night who, uniting, gave birth in their turn to Ether and Hemera. Gaea bore Uranus, the sky crowned with stars 'whom she made her equal in grandeur so that he entirely covered her'. Then she created the high mountains and 'the sterile sea' with its harmonious waves. Gaea reigned supreme before the Olympic dynasty was established; not only did this matriarchal deity create the universe and bear the race of gods but, we are informed, she created man. She was also a goddess of prophecy, the oracle of Delphi having originally belonged to her before it passed into Apollo's hands at a later date. She was venerated at Aegae, Delphi and Olympia and had sanctuaries at Dodona, Tegea, Sparta and at Athens near Areopagus.

The universe having been formed, it remained for the gods to people it. Gaea united with her son Uranus to produce the first race, the Titans. These people are not clearly defined, their name supposedly being derived from the Cretan word meaning 'king'. In Greece they were ultimately honoured as the ancestors of men and to them was attributed the invention of the arts and magic. This rather suggests that they may have had Atlantean connections, possibly a group of colonizers from the 'old country' who arrived on Greek shores in those early days and displayed cultural or scientific knowledge far ahead of their contemporaries; hence the later Prometheus tale involving the theft of fire that did not, it would seem, do much for mankind in the long run.

These early Greek legends certainly lend credence to similar stories of an advanced people who appeared as from nowhere, bringing civilization and some form of technology with them. It is surely logical to consider that anything scientific or technical would appear as 'magic' to more primitive peoples. Of course, for those who cannot accept the Atlantis theory, there is always Sumeria to fall back on, although there would not appear to be an abundance of evidence in support of the many tales related by those post-Flood historians whose observations highlighted so many of the early epics, myths and legends. The Titans, for example, have much in common with Ireland's *Tuatha de Danaans*, while the Quetzalcoatl story has a familiar ring about it. One could go on . . .

There were, we are told, twelve Titans, six male and six female, a number which is highly significant in Greek magic. They were named Oceanus, Coeus, Hyperion, Crius, Iapetus, Cronus, Theia, Rhea, Mnemosyne, Phoebe, Tethys and Themis. Uranus and Gaea then produced the Cyclopes, Brontes, Steropes and Arges, who resembled the other gods but had only one eye in the middle of their forehead. Finally they bore three monsters, Cottus, Briareus and Gyges, called the Hecatoncheires or Centimanes, whose horrific appearance so disturbed their father that as soon as they were born he shut them up in the depths of the Earth. Gaea, it seems, did not approve of this rejection of her offspring, so she planned a terrible vengeance against her spouse. From gleaming steel she fashioned a sharp sickle or *harpe* and told her children of her plan. They were all horrified and refused to co-operate, all except Cronus, her last born, who agreed to carry out the dastardly deed. When evening fell Uranus, accompanied by Night, joined his wife and unsuspectingly went to sleep. Cronus, who had been hidden in the bedchamber by his mother, then fell upon Uranus, castrated him with the sickle and cast the genitals into the sea. From the terrible wound black blood dropped and, seeping into the Earth, gave birth to the Furies, another set of monstrous giants, and to the ash tree nympths, the Meliae. The debris that floated on the surface of the waves broke into white foam from which was born the beautiful young goddess Aphrodite (foam born).

The cosmological nature of this myth naturally accords with the legends of other earlier nations, notably those of Sumeria, Mesopotamia, Asia and South America. The *Popul Vuh* tells us that 'the sea piled up and sticky substances rained from the sky'; floods and disasters are well recorded in the Babylonian Gilgamesh epic, Hebrew legends and secret

Egyptian traditions that have been handed down via occult sources over the centuries. The Chinese believed these events to have taken place in the reign of the Emperor Yaltou, during which time there was no light for days, fires and volcanoes erupted and the seas rose angrily. The Mayas tell us that the Sun god refused to give light for four days, after which a great star with a tail appeared in the sky. Doubtless all these myths, as well as the Greek story, refer to some recorded cosmological event that influenced the history of the day and no doubt affected climatic conditions throughout the globe.

This brings us to our next consideration: at what point can we divide primitive observations of natural disasters from allegory and magical knowledge?

Graves categorizes true myth as follows:

1. Philosophical allegory, as in Hesiod's cosmogony.
2. 'Aetiological' explanation of myths no longer understood, as in Admetus's yoking of a lion and a boar to his chariot.
3. Satire or parody, as in Silenus's account of Atlantis.
4. Sentimental fable, as in the story of Narcissus and Echo.
5. Embroidered history, as in Arion's adventure with the dolphin.
6. Minstrel romance, as in the story of Cephalus and Procris.
7. Political propaganda, as in Theseus's federalization of Attica.
8. Moral legend, as in the story of Eriphyle's necklace.
9. Humorous anecdote, as in the bedroom farce of Heracles, Omphale and Pan.
10. Theatrical melodrama, as in the story of Thestor and his daughters.
11. Heroic saga, as in the main argument of the *Iliad*.
12. Realistic fiction, as in Odysseus's visit to the Phaeacians.

The Greek Myths, Vol I, p. 12

It is essential for the student of magic to bear all these points in mind or he could become lost in a morass of confusing data, most of which is totally unrelated to the deeper spiritual or occult issues; but sorting the true magical wheat from the chaff of folklore, superstition and historical vagaries is always a Herculean task so, as long as this is firmly borne in mind from the onset of the study, a degree of safety may be found within its logic.

Those readers who wish to refer to the finer details of Greek mythology are recommended to peruse the works of Robert Graves or Professor Carl Kerenyi, in whose scholarship they may indulge to their heart's content. Here we are dealing primarily with an occult analysis and not with a study of the classics, so let us return once again to those early characters whose nature and function carry some degree of magical or psychological significance.

The Titan Iapetus had four sons: Menoetius, Atlas, Prometheus and Epimetheus. Menoetius and Atlas were punished by Zeus for their part in the Titans' revolt, Menoetius being despatched to darkest Erebus while Atlas was condemned to stand before the Hesperides on the edge of the world and bear the vault of heaven on his shoulders. Prometheus, whose main weapon would appear to have been cunning, had a different fate and played an important role in the legendary history and origins of humanity; during the revolt of the Titans he kept a prudent neutrality and was actually admitted into the circle of immortals, but he entertained a silent grudge against the destroyers of his race and constantly favoured men against the gods.

Robert Graves postulates that the Talmudic archangel Michael was the counterpart of Prometheus, no doubt on account of the similarity between the story of Prometheus using clay and water to fashion the first men in the likeness of gods into whom Athene breathed life, and the story of Jehovah acting in a similar fashion to create Adam and then Eve, the latter having points in common with Pandora, as we shall see. Obviously both stories came from the same source. Greek philosophers distinguished Promethean man from the imperfect Earth-born creation, part of which was destroyed by Zeus and the rest washed away in the Deucalionian Flood, in much the same way that Genesis Ch. 6 talks of 'sons of God' and 'daughters of men' as if they were different races or species. Some of the earlier Greek accounts would also appear to have been borrowed from the Gilgamesh epic, notably in the writings of Ovid.

Prometheus, whose name is said to mean 'forethought' and

'swastika', was reputed to have given men the gift of fire which he stole from the forge of Hephaestus. Outraged by the theft, Zeus, who was already thoroughly angered by Prometheus constantly favouring men against the gods, ordered Hephaestus to fashion clay and water into a body of great beauty that would equal an immortal goddess, at least in appearance. All the divinities bestowed gifts upon this creature who was called Pandora, except Hermes whose offering consisted of a warped mind. Zeus then sent her as a gift to Epimetheus and, although Prometheus had warned his brother against accepting gifts from Olympus, Epimetheus was dazzled by her beauty, welcomed her and made a place for her amongst men. Pandora carried in her arms a great vase, incorrectly called her 'box'. When she raised the lid all the terrible afflictions with which it had been filled escaped and spread across the Earth among mankind. Only Hope did not fly away.

Zeus, it seems, was still not pacified so he resolved to annihilate the human race with a deluge. But once again Prometheus lent his aid to mankind by warning his son Deucalion who, on the advice of his father, constructed an ark in which to take refuge when the waters rose. For nine days and nine nights Deucalion and his wife floated on the risen tides, but on the tenth day the downpour ceased and the two survivors were able to disembark on the crest of Mount Othrys or Mount Parnassus. Deucalion offered up a sacrifice to Zeus; the god, touched by his piety, promised to grant him his first wish and Deucalion requested the renewal of the human race.

Although peace had been concluded between Zeus and mankind, Prometheus was made to suffer severely for his trickery and thefts; his agonies, which are well documented in the myths, were finally assuaged when he was released by Hercules at a later date.

The occult significance of this story is obvious; it concerns the ever recurring theme of a group of people who possessed advanced knowledge of both science and magic which they gave to a race who were not spiritually or somatically evolved enough to make good use of it. The Tree of Knowledge inevitably carries its sacrificed saviour, Prometheus joining the ranks of those wisdom gods who suffered for the redemption of mankind but also gained knowledge and furthered their own spiritual evolution as a result.

The story of the Flood appears in the myths and legends of many lands although, perhaps, the Biblical version and Plato's story of Atlantis are probably the best known. The rescue of Prometheus by Hercules (Heracles) indicates man's ability to free himself from the karmic wheel through initiation and inner understanding; in other words, through the quest of the Heroic Path.

Equal occult significance lies in the next piece of 'myth' we shall examine, namely the four (some say five) ages of man. The first men, we are told, who were contemporaries of Cronus, enjoyed complete happiness in the Golden Age. Hesiod tells us that they lived like gods, free from worry and fatigue; old age did not afflict them and, they rejoiced in continual festivity. They were not immortal but they died peacefully as though in 'sweet slumber'. All the blessings of the world were theirs; the fruitful Earth gave forth its treasures unbidden and the people ate fruit and honey and drank the milk of goats. After their death the people of the Golden Age became benevolent genii, protectors and tutelary guardians of the living. They bestowed good fortune, were the patrons of music and helped men to uphold justice if their spiritual advice was heard and followed.

Next came the Silver Age which was matriarchal. Although these people tended to be quarrelsome and subject to their womenfolk, it did not appear to do them much harm as they lived to be a hundred years old or more. They did not make war or kill each other; neither did they offer blood sacrifices; and they were good agriculturalists. They have been equated with the Minoans by some experts, but more generally with the early European goddess worshippers already mentioned. Legend has it that Zeus destroyed them.

These people were followed by a Brazen or Bronze race who 'fell like fruit from Ash Trees'. Their men were robust and delighted only in oaths, meat eating and warlike exploits. 'Their pitiless hearts were hard as steel, their might was untameable and their arms invincible.' According to one source they ended by cutting each other's throats, while another account has it that 'black death' seized them all; these were our invaders from the north who worked in bronze, no doubt, the ash tree (Yggdrasil) being a highly significant symbol in their system of religious belief.

After the Bronze Age Hesiod places the Heroic Age, peopled by valiant warriors begotten by the gods of mortal mothers. They fought before Thebes and under the walls of Troy; they were the heroes of Greece who dwelt in the Elysian Fields. But the more widespread opinion was that the Bronze Age was followed by the Iron Age, or contemporary age, a period of misery, crime, treachery and cruelty 'when men respect neither their vows, nor justice, nor virtue'. This explanation is said to account for the progressive degeneracy of man.

Our own comment is that we are obviously part of the latter age and can only cling to the pious hope that through the Heroic Path of trial and labour we will complete the circle and return once again to the Golden Age of enlightenment, happiness, understanding and love.

2. THE OLYMPIAN TAKE-OVER

After Cronus had reduced his father Uranus to impotence he liberated his brothers the Titans — with the exception of the Cyclopes and Hecatoncheires — and set himself up as chief of the new dynasty. Creation continued with many more deities, mortals and fabulous beasts assuming identity. These are far too numerous to describe in this work and no doubt constitute a hotch-potch of religious allegory, nature energies and rulers who came and went. We can pick up the story at the point where Cronus mated with his sister, Rhea, who gave him three daughters — Hestia, Demeter and Hera; and three sons — Hades, Poseidon and Zeus.

An oracular prediction that Cronus would one day be overthrown by one of his children caused him great concern, so much in fact that he felt obliged to swallow each of them as they were born. Rhea was overwhelmed with grief and questioned why it should be her destiny to part with her offspring in this peculiar fashion. When her time approached to give birth to Zeus she sought the help of her own parents, Uranus and Gaea, to save the child. On their advice she travelled to Crete and brought forth her son in a deep cavern in the forests of Mount Aegeum. Gaea looked after the child, while Rhea wrapped up a large stone in swaddling clothes and presented it to Cronus who immediately swallowed it.

Gaea carried her grandson to Mount Ida (or Mount Dicte) where he was cared for by two nymphs, Ida and Adrasteia, and entertained by the Curetes. Some scholars claim the latter to have been a primitive tribe of the region, but the general opinion is that they were earth spirits or nature energies. Later they were deified for their services to the father of the gods and temples were erected to them, notably at Messina.

Sheltered from his father's ire, Zeus grew to manhood in the forests of Ida. His wet nurse was the goat Amaltheia, a wondrous beast of whom even immortals went in awe. In gratitude Zeus placed her among the constellations and from her hide, which no arrow could pierce, the aegis was fashioned. To the nymphs he gave one of her horns which contained an inexhaustible supply of whatever food or drink was desired. This became the famous cornucopia or horn of plenty, a symbol which also appears in the legends and magical systems of many other pantheons.

The oracle that had made the prediction to Cronus had not lied. Upon reaching manhood Zeus planned to punish his father; according to Apollodorus, the god summoned Metis to his aid and she administered to Cronus a draught which caused him to vomit the stone, plus his own children whom he had swallowed. Vanquished by his son's might the old god was driven from the sky and despatched to some far-flung corner of the universe, at least according to the Homeric account, but other sources insist that he was sent to the ends of the Earth to dwell in bliss, or plunged into mysterious slumber in Thule. Zeus placed the stone Cronus had disgorged at the foot of Mount Parnassus to bear witness to his victory and 'to be one day in the eyes of mortals a monument to these wonders'. This famous stone was preserved at Delphi for many years. The era of the Olympians had begun.

In the story of the mutilation of Uranus the message must surely be that an epoch in the development and evolution of Earth was brought to an end by the passage of time, after which a gentle and more enlightened age (the Golden Age) emerged. Moving on once again, the oracular prediction regarding the eventual overthrow of Cronus would appear to suggest that certain far-sighted persons, anticipating the onset of a new order, strove to suppress the oncoming tide of development, much of which appeared to them to be negative and retrogressive. The stone represented encapsulated energy which, when released, initiated the next age. Occultly it is necessary to consider time as an energy or power in its own right, which the people of the Golden Age of Cronus understood and were able to manipulate. With the departure of the old god his energies were withdrawn and this knowledge was lost; the new race who assumed supremacy, being warlike and materialistic, lacked the scientific or magical know-how of their predecessors. The next episode in our little drama will serve to throw even more light onto this area of study.

The Titans, with the exception of Oceanus, were jealous of the Olympians and wished to regain their status by reconquering the kingdom of which they had been dispossessed. A dreadful battle between the gods and the Titans ensued which resulted in the latter being finally defeated, bound in chains and cast into the depths of the Earth. Here we see the final downfall or end of those beings, whoever they might have been, who were the teachers and allies of mankind. The records suggest a cosmological drama, involving natural phenomena, which preceded the eventual Flood.

The struggle with the Titans was followed by a war with the giants. The giants had sprung from the blood of the mutilated Uranus and were distinguished by other features as well as their size. But the gods alone were unable to triumph over these monstrosities and needed the help of a mortal man. This man was Hercules, whose escapades we shall consider later in this narrative.

Many early records abound with stories of giants or people of considerably larger size than present day *Homo sapiens*. According to the Bible 'there were giants in the earth in those days' and one only needs to refer to some of the mammoth structures scattered around the Earth for confirmation of the wide coverage this belief received.

It is conceivable that during the early days of this planet's evolution there were races contemporary, perhaps, with the Saurians, which were latterly rendered extinct in some major cataclysm described in the myths in terms of a war between Heaven and Earth. In his book *Atlantis and the Giants* the French scholar Denis Saurat postulated that the size and height of people could be determined by the gravitational pull of the Moon, any slight alteration involving distances between the Earth, its satellite and the rest of the solar system being highly significant in the growth factor. No doubt his hypothesis will not meet with the approval of many, but the concept of unsuspected mutations occurring between prototype man and *Homo sapiens* as we know him today is certainly worth consideration.

More time cannot be spent on the detail accompanying these legends, however, and it is important from a magical standpoint that we aim to analyse our prime target: the Olympians, their nature and deeds.

Under Zeus the immortals formed a society with its own laws and hierarchy. First came twelve great gods and goddesses: Zeus, Poseidon, Hephaestus, Hermes, Ares and Apollo; Hera, Artemis, Hestia, Athene, Aphrodite and Demeter. Other divinities, such as Helios, Selene, Leto, Dione, Dionysus, Themis and Eros, shared the Olympic heights. The courtiers of the Olympians, sworn in their service, were the Horae, the Moerae, Nemesis, the Graces, the Muses, Iris, Hebe and Ganymede. Hades, although brother of Zeus, did not reside on Olympus where his brother was in command, but chose to dwell with his ladies, Persephone and Hecate, in his own subterranean empire.

An arrangement had been made between Zeus and his brothers that each had his own territory: Zeus the sky; Poseidon the seas and waters; and Hades the underworld. Although from time to time territorial disputes involving immortals, heroes and mortals did arise, for the most part the brothers each kept his side of the bargain.

There was only one power to whom Zeus was subject and that was Moros, or destiny. But Aphrodite's famous girdle was also a protection against the thunderbolts of Zeus and, if she chose to deflect his shafts with this magical aid, even the father of the gods could not win: a valid pointer to the real power behind the love ray in its purest form.

The Olympians were credited with human passions and qualities. Love, hatred, anger and envy were known to them and they cruelly punished anyone who questioned their authority or upset them in any way; but equally they showered favours on those who revered and honoured them with gifts. Here we have a clear indication of a culture that imposed terrestrial values upon their heaven and its resident deities. They saw the gods in their own image and likeness, just as many people in our present day and age are inclined to visualize 'God' in some patriarchal form that accords with the customs and culture in which they have been raised. It is in this aspect that the Greek and early Egyptian religious concepts diverge; the Egyptians were able to accept a supreme deity in forms other than their own, or even in the abstract. This could have been due to the stronger influence imposed upon their infant culture by those 'outsiders' who left such an indelible imprint on their ethos.

3. THE PANTHEON OF TWELVE

Let us now consider the Olympians individually and analyse their nature and qualities in a metaphysical light.

Zeus

According to Larousse, the name Zeus contains the Sanskrit root *dyaus* and the Latin *dies* (the day), suggesting the luminous sky. Zeus was therefore ruler of the sky and all atmospheric phenomena. The winds, the clouds, the beneficial rain, and the destructive thunder and lightning came under his command. Being 'all high' he was venerated in lofty places such as mountain tops. He had his own oracle at Dodona but occasionally borrowed the use of Delphi from Apollo. The oak tree was sacred to him for obvious reasons and he is often depicted wearing a crown of oak leaves. He is considered by some authorities to have originated as a solar deity on account of his sanctuary in Arcadia on Mount Lycaeus, the root of the word *lycaeus* meaning 'light'.

Zeus is shown as a man in the fullness of maturity, of robust body, with thick dark waving or curling hair and a beard. He wears a long mantle which leaves his chest and right arm free; the sceptre is in his left hand and the thunderbolt and eagle at his feet. His magical colour is imperial purple.

Before Zeus installed Hera as first lady of Olympus he had several earlier unions, the first of which was to Metis (wisdom) who, Hesiod tells us, knew more things than all the gods and men together. Gaea and Uranus warned Zeus that if he had children by Metis they would be more powerful than he and eventually dethrone him. So, when Metis was about to give birth to Athene, in order to forestall this hazard Zeus swallowed the mother and her unborn child, thus avoiding any future problems and at the same time embodying wisdom.

His next wife was Themis, daughter of Uranus and Gaea. Themis represented the law which regulates both physical and moral order. Her children were the Horae or seasons, Eunomia (wise legislation), Dike (justice), Eirene (peace) and finally the Fates or Moerae, sometimes referred to as daughters of Night. Even when she was replaced by Hera, Themis continued to remain near Zeus as adviser; hence her place among the immortals in Olympus.

Zeus eventually married Hera, although their relationship had been a long established one. There are many legends concerning this divine courtship, the best known of which is probably Pausanias's account of Zeus visiting his sister in the form of a cuckoo in distress upon which the kindly Hera took pity. Renowned for getting his own amorous way, Zeus promptly changed back to his Olympian form to claim the fulfilment of his desire. Hera, however, resisted and it was not until he promised to marry her that she finally succumbed to his advances. Although the wedding ceremony was solemnly celebrated on Olympus, this by no means put an end to Zeus's inclinations and, in spite of Hera's jealousy and constant efforts to thwart her husband's *affaires*, he continued to pursue both goddesses and mortal women alike.

One could write a book solely about Zeus's exploits but at present we are considering the esoteric implications of his nature and deeds. Zeus represented those patriarchal energies that swamped the previously matriarchal lands of the old goddess, their manifestation being the imposition of the male will over the female by sheer physical strength. Under the former regime women had ruled by intuitive guidance, the utilization of natural Earth powers, agriculture and general fertility. The conquering races saw things in a different light, however, their aggressive rulers being able to take whom they wished when they wished, by brute force, in their amorous pursuit. Zeus himself represented masculine energy in its kingly mode for, as well as being something of an effective 'stud', the god was also a fair giver of law and order. It is not surprising, therefore, that his influence is associated with the planet Jupiter in astrology since he appears as a bastion of the establishment and a sort of 'Edward VII' character, loved by many in spite of his obvious 'human' traits.

The Zeus energies manifest through the much sought after qualities of justice, leadership, popularity and charisma, one of many good reasons why the Olympian system of Greek magic could play an important role in our modern world.

Hera

Originally her name was said to be derived from the Latin word for master — *herus* — and an old Greek word meaning 'earth'; but now it is thought to be connected with the Sanskrit word *svar* (the sky). So, like her celestial spouse, she was a deity of the upper regions of the air. Her esoteric attributes were soon forgotten among a people who were nothing if not 'earth-earthy', so she was designated patroness of marriage and all phases of feminine life.

Hera is depicted as a woman of severe beauty and nobility; she wears a veil and is well clothed as befits the modesty of a matron. Her symbols are the sceptre surmounted by the cuckoo, a pomegranate — representing conjugal love and fruitfulness — and the peacock. Her daughter Hebe is often shown beside her mother.

Hera represents womanly stability in a male orientated society, her only line of defence being her marital status and — let's face it — such has been the lot of women of her kind since the dawn of the Fourth/Fifth Age. The cuckoo story is typical of so many ladies who trapped their men into marriage by becoming pregnant. Hera is the faithful wife and mother, always hovering in the background but, nevertheless, angered by her husband's infidelities.

Jung divided women into four main archetypal categories: Mary, the mother; Eve, the temptress; Helen, the heroine; and Sophia, the intellectual. This theme is re-echoed by Edward Whitmont in his book *The Symbolic Quest* in which he suggests that all women unconsciously identify themselves with the mother, the *hetaira* or courtesan, the Amazon, or the medium. Hera's place in both these categorizations is obvious.

The stories of Zeus and Hera are, as with many of the gods, too numerous to recount in this work and not all relevant to the heroic quest, so we will abridge our script accordingly.

Athene

When Zeus swallowed his wife Metis she was heavy with child. Shortly afterwards the god was afflicted with a dreadful headache and sought the aid of Hephaestus (or Prometheus according to some accounts) who split his skull with a bronze axe to relieve the pain. As the wound opened, out sprang Athene shouting a triumphant cry of victory, fully armed and brandishing a sharp javelin. Both Heaven and Earth were awestruck by the miracle, it seems, and the 'bright-eyed goddess' assumed a special place in all hearts.

Athene was a warrior goddess and not even Ares, god of war, could match her in battle. She wore a golden helmet and over her shoulder was slung the aegis, which had been fashioned from the hide of the goat Amaltheia. The finished product came in the form of a breastplate or cuirass, fringed and bordered with snakes, with the horrifying head of the Gorgon in the centre. In the Trojan wars she sided with Greece and eventually entered into the affray personally, felling the mighty Ares with a blow from her magic spear.

She also patronized heroes and protected the brave and valiant and many were the favours she conferred upon Hercules during the period of his trials. She was essentially a virgin goddess — some achievement amongst the Don Juans of the time — and highly skilled in certain domestic crafts. Weaving and embroidery were two arts in which she excelled and the finished articles were available for those immortals and mortals who pleased her. She was extremely jealous of her skill in this field, however, as illustrated in the story of Arachne.

Areas in which she could also bestow benefits were healing and health, and she is credited with inventing the flute. In addition to the tools of the warrior her emblem was the owl and she was universally acknowledged as the goddess of wisdom.

There is something of the Egyptian Hathor in Athene's nature. Hathor also played a dual role, Sekhmet being her warrior *persona* and her alter-ego the nourishing and domesticated patroness of women.

Athene could be generous to those who impressed her; the aid and benefits she bestowed upon the heroes emphasize the esoteric truth that wisdom is an essential prerequisite for the successful negotiation of the ordeals and initiations of the Heroic Path, physical strength alone being insufficient. The portrayal of the warrior archetype in female form is itself occultly significant, the indication being that the 'Sophia' or wisdom aspect of woman can sometimes exert a more civilizing influence than the physically stronger and more logically orientated male principle which dominates today's world. But time holds the key to wisdom's final victory (as the Egyptians so wisely observed in the nature of their god Thoth/Tehuti) and we have not yet reached that point in our evolutionary cycle at which the final act of the drama will be witnessed.

Apollo

It has been suggested that the etymology of Apollo's name is uncertain. The old Greek verb meaning 'to repel or set aside' is one explanation and another links it with the English word 'apple'. The latter is interesting in the light of Bob Stewart's book, *Who Was St George?*, which suggests more than one correspondence between the British pantheons and the Horus/Apollo figures of Egyptian and Greek mythology. Because of his connection with the Hyperboreans he is also thought of as a Nordic divinity, brought by the Greeks from the north during the course of their migrations. There are many question marks in the classics concerning Apollo, notably his role in the Trojan war, which we will leave for the scholars to argue out amongst themselves.

Apollo was above all things a solar or light god. He was the son of Leto and twin brother of Artemis. Leto was the daughter of Croeus and Phoebe and a former mate of Zeus. When pregnant with his children, Leto was pursued by Hera and wandered the Earth seeking a place to rest herself and give birth; but, as Hera's fury was so great, none would assist or receive her. Hera decreed that she could only give birth in a place where the Sun's rays never penetrated; so, in order that this command should not be disobeyed, Poseidon raised the waves like a dome over the island of Ortygia, at the same time anchoring it in the depths of the sea with four pillars. After Apollo's birth the island's name was changed to Delos, 'the brilliant'.

Hera did everything she could to delay the birth by keeping Ilithyia, goddess of childbirth, out of the way, so for nine days and nights Leto suffered atrociously. Finally Iris went to Olympus and fetched Ilithyia for her and Leto was able to produce first Artemis and then Apollo.

Even during his childhood the exploits of Apollo were many and his infant encounter with the serpent Python echoes earlier myths. But most of all Apollo is known for his oracle at Delphi. How he came to acquire this site is a story in itself and involves some seafaring folk whom he approached in the form of a dolphin; he persuaded them to settle in harsh Pytho and invoke his aid as 'the Delphinian'. As we have already explained, other deities made earlier claims to the Delphic oracle, but it was probably under Apollo's protection and tutelage that it thrived. Doubtless there is an Earth 'energy source', or power centre, in the area that stimulates the right hemisphere of the brain, or the *Ajna* chakra perhaps, which could be tapped by anyone possessing the correct magical 'know how'.

Apollo was the celestial archer whose arrows were infallible; he was god of musicians — the lyre being his instrument — patron of prophecy, representative of all forms of art and beauty and beloved brother of Artemis. He is depicted as a handsome golden-haired youth, athletic and perfectly proportioned. His constant companions were the Muses, about whom we shall speak in a later chapter. Occultly he represented the solar force in all its aspects.

Artemis

Twin sister of the Sun god, Artemis was goddess of the chase and of forests. Because of one of her symbols, the bear, she is often confused with Callisto and, rather like the Egyptian Horus, there were several (earlier) versions of her archetype, notably the fertility goddess of Ephesus. Artemis was worshipped as an agricultural deity in Arcadia and some connect her with the Celtic goddess of Berne whose symbol was also a she-bear. As her brother was to the Sun, so was Artemis to the Moon, but she is not solely a lunar deity.

Artemis was, like Athene, a virgin goddess and she showed no mercy to any being who dared attempt to violate her person. Legend has it that only once did she fall in love and that was with Orion, the hunter. Her brother, to whom she was very close, was jealous of this affection and contrived, by a trick, to cause his sister accidentally to shoot her loved one. Both children loved their mother and spared no effort to protect Leto in times of danger or distress.

When she was born Artemis approached her father with a request for eternal virginity; a bow and arrow like Apollo's; the office of bringing light; and a saffron hunting tunic. Animals generally were sacred to her, but she had little patience with people at times and severely punished those who made a nuisance of themselves or refused to abide by the laws of her domains. One of the translations of her name is said to mean 'safe and sound' or 'she who heals sickness'. Another gentle trait in her legendary character was a love of music and she had a good singing voice. As *Artemis Hymnia* she rejoiced in song and dance and would sing while her brother accompanied her on the lyre.

Artemis is represented carrying a torch, which is more solar than lunar in character. Her form is that of a young virgin, slim and supple, beautiful in a severe way; her garment is short, her feet are shod and she is accompanied by an animal, usually a dog or hind. The old Artemis of Ephesus was quite different, however, having more in common with the pre-Hellenic mother goddesses whose nature was decidedly lunar. Because of the trials her mother underwent prior to and during her birth, she presided over childbirth, together with Ilythyia, and she is also protector of women against personal violation. Her healing powers are more of a mental than a physical nature, in spite of the rugged out-of-doors type of *persona* bestowed upon her by the Greeks, while her brother presides over the curing of physical injuries.

Both Apollo and Artemis were hunters and skilled in marksmanship. There is a deeply esoteric meaning to this particular archetype: the hunter hunts for souls, his or her 'prey' representing a spiritual goal. The bow and arrow therefore carry profound occult significance in the Greek system; they represent the positive and negative aspects of the personality, the *anima/animus*, which need to be stretched to their finest tension before the 'target' can be achieved. The Greeks equated Apollo and Artemis with the Egyptian deities Horus and Bast and there are many similarities, although Bast is somewhat gentler in character than Arcadian Artemis, especially in her domestic mode, while Apollo assumes far more human attributes than his Egyptian counterpart. But then one has to take into account the fact that any archetype will be coloured and reclothed according to the nature of the indigenous population and afterwards remodelled by the religious fashions and political designs of successive generations of conquerors.

Hermes

Earlier times saw Hermes in the pastoral role. In fact he can be traced back to Pelasgian and Thracian origins and was greatly honoured by the shepherds of Arcadia; but he was also associated with movement, action, and the wind or Element of Air. All kinds of profit, lawful and unlawful, came under his rulership, as well as games of chance. With the growth and development of the classical Greek pantheon Hermes assumed the role of patron of travellers, or the early Greek equivalent of the modern day St Christopher. Like the Egyptian Anubis he was sometimes considered as *psychopompus* or conductor of souls, and there would appear to be points at which the two archetypes blend. Travel and commerce were certainly his scene, as were learning and all forms of mental activity and agility. As messenger to the gods he assumes certain of the qualities of the Biblical angels, but the delicacy of some of his Olympic missions also hints at the gifts of diplomacy and tact.

Hermes is represented in the athletic mode, as would befit a divine runner. His body is shown as lithe and graceful, his hair is short and crisp, and his attitude is of one who is listening and learning. Mostly he wears a round, winged hat or *petasus* and his feet are shod with winged sandals. In his hand he holds the caduceus, the insignia of the medical profession, which symbolizes the balance necessary for good health and well being.

The emblems of Hermes are highly significant and speak more for his occult role than the many stories of his deeds. He is credited with the invention of the lyre which he gave to Apollo in return for the caduceus, together with some sheep he had supposedly stolen from the Sun god. Here we have an exchange of energies between two major archetypes, Apollo bestowing his medical skills upon Hermes and in return assuming a more artistic and musical role. In other words, the story is telling us that in the Greek pantheon the healing powers of the Sun are passed from the instinctive or natural therapeutic modes to the logical and reasoning approach that is so much a part of the Greek nature and character. Hermes' practical medical skill is underlined in his replacing of Zeus's severed nerves which had been cut by the monster Typhoeus during the period when he held the great god in captivity. Hermes' son, Pan, was also a healing deity, but after Pan's alleged 'death' the healing energies of nature which he represented became absorbed into the more rational Greek ethos, with Hermes assuming the overall healing role.

Ares

Ares' name would appear to indicate his nature in more than one tongue. The Sanskrit root *mar* gave birth to the Vedic *maruts*, or storm divinities, while the Greek root means to 'carry away or destroy'. Originally of Thracian origin, Ares was not the nicest of characters, it would seem. In addition to a predilection for combat for its own sake he had a rather nasty temper and his squires, Demos and Phobos (fear and fright) plus Eris (strife), naturally did not endear him to people. As he represented blind energy and uncontrolled passion, Athene was his natural enemy since her martial skills were coupled with wisdom and intelligence, so the angry Ares hardly had a chance against her. Needless to say, Ares was not the happiest of lovers either. Although he managed to interest Aphrodite in his advances purely on the ground of his manly attributes, he was caught in the act by Hephaestus, which tale will shortly be told. Aphrodite bore him a daughter, Harmonia, a clear esoteric message that love can tame force and bring harmony.

Ares is shown as a hefty warrior wearing a crested helmet. But, apart from the obvious associations with raw, untamed energy, he has no specific symbols or attributes and even his military associations are somewhat dubious. However, he was one of the Olympians and how his archetype is handled by the aspiring Hero is highly important to those who would pursue the Greek occult path, 'discipline' being the operative word.

Hephaestus

Smith gods appeared in the pantheons of most of the early cultures. Agni was the Vedic god of fire and hearth; Britain had its Wayland; Egypt its Ptah, the master craftsman; and so forth. There is a 'gnomey' quality about Hephaestus which brings him in line with those archetypes who are rather unprepossessing in appearance but highly gifted. According to Homer poor Hephaestus was actually born lame, although some sources insist that he received his injury in another way. His mother, Hera, appalled by his deformity, threw him from the heights but his creative skills soon took him back there again.

Hephaestus managed to gain the love goddess herself as a bride. Needless to say, this caused him a few Olympian headaches but he contrived to keep her in the end, in spite of the advances she received from a whole host of gods, godlings, heroes and mortals. Love and creativity, it would seem, go hand in hand.

All the gods and goddesses had recourse to Hephaestus's skills at different times, his craftsmanship being unquestionably the best there was around Olympus or anywhere else. He could also use this to his own advantage, as may be evidenced in the story of his famous net. Suspecting his wife of infidelity, he forged a net so fine that it could not be seen yet so strong that it could not be broken. As Aphrodite shared her couch with Ares, Hephaestus stole up on the couple and waited for them to fall asleep, whereupon he spread the net over them and invited the whole company of Olympus to come and see how he had been treated. Some of the gods sniggered at the sight, while several of the goddesses were downright shocked or affronted, but more at the invasion of privacy than in prudishness. Zeus finally persuaded him to let them go after extracting a promise from Ares to pay the price of his adultery. One rather suspects that the Greeks were pointing out the folly of washing one's dirty linen in public! Hephaestus's famous net, however, became an important magical tool, the use of which will be explained in a later chapter.

The lame smith god is depicted as short and swarthy, the upper part of his body appearing almost too heavy for his legs. On his head he wears a conical bonnet and in his hands he holds the hammer and tongs, both highly potent occult symbols.

Aphrodite

The story of Uranus has already furnished us with the legend of the birth of this goddess from the 'foam', although Homer describes her as the daughter of Zeus and Dione. Aphrodite corresponds to several other deities such as the Babylonian Ishtar and the Norse Freya. One source suggests that her name is a feminine form of Zeus, rather indicating an ill-defined personality of debatable origin. The answer probably lies in the fact that the love principle was so strongly acknowledged by the people that a character had to be built up around it.

Aphrodite was the classic beautiful woman, fair-haired, blue-eyed, voluptuous: Jung's 'Eve', the temptress and archetypal sex symbol. She was capable of arousing passionate desires in anyone in whom it pleased and amused her to so do. With the exception of Athene, Artemis and Hestia, all gods, heroes and mortals yielded to her power, although on occasions she received a dose of her own medicine, as with her Anchises adventure, Zeus being the culprit in that instance.

The goddess of love had her own retinue, the best known character of which was undoubtedly Eros. Considered by many to be purely a personification of a cosmic force, his role was to co-ordinate the elements of which the universe is composed. Eros brought harmony to chaos, thus permitting the continual development of life. There is little agreement as to his origins and several parents have been allotted to him. The popular concept, however, is of Aphrodite in the maternal role constantly having to punish her offspring for causing so much havoc among gods and men. He is depicted as a winged child with a bow and arrow, the darts of which 'fire passion in all hearts at which they are aimed'. It is little wonder that this archetype ended up with the goddess of love herself, as his association with both fecundity and erotic love is obvious.

Aphrodite was also accompanied by the Graces, who were fathered on the Oceanid Eurynome by Zeus. These were happy, pleasant divinities whose presence spread joy, sweetness and charm. Although given many names by various early writers, they are generally accepted as being Aglaia, Euphrosyne and Thalia. As companions to the goddess they attended her *toilette* and aided in her adornment for special occasions.

The Graces were probably nature deities originally,

associated with the spring or summer. Aglaia was called 'the brilliant'; Euphrosyne, 'she who rejoices the heart'; and Thalia, 'she who brought flowers'. Magically speaking they represent the natural beauty that attends pure love, bringing joy and gladness to all who experience it.

Aphrodite's most potent occult symbol was undoubtedly her girdle which was strong enough to halt even the thunderbolts of Zeus himself, a sure indication that love is ultimately the most powerful force in the universe.

Poseidon

Poseidon was traditionally lord of the sea. The Greeks saw him as the brother of Zeus although, according to other sources, he pre-dated Zeus, being an old Pelasgian deity whose influence had filtered through from primitive times.

Although a member of the godly company of Olympus, Poseidon was always subject to his brother's sovereign authority. Naturally the old chap complained from time to time, but having charge of not only the sea but also all lakes, rivers and waterways he was presented with many opportunities to take his revenge.

There are some very interesting magical connotations associated with this god; his transport, for example. One depiction shows him riding in a chariot drawn by Tritons blowing conch shells, but in the more popular representation his carriage is 'drawn by white steeds with golden manes and shod in bronze'. The cult of the white horse has such strong connections with Poseidon that the suggestion of a link with the Celtic goddess Epona cannot be ignored. In addition to the white horse, all marine life was sacred to him and his magical symbol was the trident. The stories of his nature and deeds emphasize the power of the Element of Water; but as his kingdoms were subject to the ultimate authority of Zeus, lord of air, the message must surely be that intellect is the stronger force in the long run, head being the better judge than heart.

Hestia

The Greek word *hestia* means hearth, the place in the house where fire was burned, food was cooked and from which warmth and comfort were derived. Fire was very important to primitive people in more ways than one, as it provided a dialogue between men and gods via the sacrificial flames. Hestia was therefore a fiery goddess, like Hephaestus. But her fire was of the domestic sort, around which the family could gather to find togetherness and continuity. The circle was sacred to Hestia and her temples were always characterized by this form. Her origins are obscure and neither Hesiod nor Homer appear to be familiar with her. She was a virgin goddess who chose a modest existence in spite of the splendour of Olympus. Her mien was one of reserved dignity and repose, which served to contrast her with the more robust or flamboyant female Olympians. Although unmarried and a virgin, Hestia protected the hearth and home and ensured continuity and stability in all matters in which she was invoked. She is depicted sometimes seated, sometimes standing, but always still, tranquil and of modest demeanour.

Demeter

Goddess of the soil and all growing things, Demeter had much in common with the old mother goddesses Gaea and Rhea, her name being derived from the root words for 'earth' and 'mother' which naturally connected her with the Underworld and all growing things issuing from the soil. In Arcadia she was depicted with a horse's head and bearing in one hand a dolphin and in the other a dove. The Greeks themselves linked her with the Egyptian Isis, but the horse's head could also put her in line with the Celtic horse goddesses.

Magically Demeter is highly interesting. Her temples were often found in forests and were called 'megara'. They became associated with secret rites and orgies and, of course, the famous Eleusinia; but it is in her maternal aspect that she is best known, appearing as a somewhat sad-looking, golden-haired lady crowned with ears of corn or a ribbon and holding either a sceptre, ears of corn, or a torch.

The story of Demeter and her beloved daughter Kore is well known. Hades, brother of Zeus, snatched the maiden while she was out picking flowers one day and claimed her as his bride, Zeus apparently having given his permission for this deed. Many were the trials of poor Demeter while she strove to reclaim her daughter and, because of her distress, she withdrew her energies so that nothing would grow on Earth and both gods and men were forced to plead with her to restore her bounty. Demeter was adamant; she would not permit the Earth to bear fruit until she had seen her daughter again. Zeus eventually sent Hermes to Hades with a request to return the maiden who had been renamed Persephone. Hades grudgingly complied but managed to persuade her to eat a few pomegranate seeds beforehand, these being the symbol of marriage, which permanently sealed the union. When once again she fell into her mother's arms Demeter questioned her as to whether she had eaten anything while within Hades' domains because, 'If thou hast not eaten thou shalt live with me on Olympus. But if thou hast, then thou must return to the depths of the Earth.' Poor Persephone admitted that she had eaten the pomegranate seeds, much to Demeter's chagrin, but as a compromise Zeus decided that Persephone should dwell one-third of the year with her husband and the remaining two-thirds with her mother. Demeter settled for this bargain and once again the Earth brought forth fruit in abundance and all things flourished. Before she returned to Olympus Demeter taught her divine science to the leaders of men, thus initiating them into her sacred Mysteries, the Eleusinia, which will be dealt with in a separate chapter.

* * *

These twelve Olympians and their respective retinues were woven from the fabric of older themes and fashioned by those cultures that affected the prevailing influence of the times. New pantheons are usually formed from the remnants of older ones; a healthy probe into the psychology of those who accepted and propagated them can give the occult seeker a fair degree of insight into the archetypal manifestations appropriate to the period in world history, general evolutionary trends and contributory imprint of the ethos in question. Without a shadow of doubt civilization over the ensuing centuries owes much to the cultural, logical, albeit hidden magical influence of the denizens of Mount Olympus and their creators.

4. THE MINOR DEITIES

The Greek pantheons abound with lesser gods and godlings, not all of which carry a strong magical influence as far as the Olympian system is concerned. But as there will undoubtedly be many pursuants of the Heroic Path who may feel drawn to seek their tutelary services, a few of the more prominent personalities are deserving of mention.

Divinities of the Underworld

Hades
While many may classify Hades as a major deity, he functions outside the main Olympian magical stream, although the regions over which he ruled do play an important role in the Greek mystical scene. In his own domains, the Underworld, Hades was absolute master. He was perfectly happy in this subterranean environment and only surfaced on two occasions: to abduct Persephone, and to seek healing for a wound inflicted upon him by Hercules. He wore a helmet which rendered him invisible, so if and when he did choose to take the odd earthly jaunt, none but the initiated would observe his presence. Hades was also known by the name of Pluto, from the Greek word *plouton* meaning wealth or riches, an aspect of his nature which obviously alludes to the treasures to be found deep within the Earth itself. So it is little wonder that his good offices were sought for material gain

rather than in his role as ruler of the chthonic regions.

Hecate

Originally a Thracian Moon goddess, Hecate is often confused with Artemis as her name is said to derive from a feminine form of one of the titles of Apollo — the 'far-darter'. She is usually considered as the third member of the triple Moon goddess unit in which she represents the crone, Artemis being the maiden and Demeter the mother (or Aphrodite, the nubile woman, depending on the specific triplicity). Her power embraced both the sky and the Earth and the gifts she bestowed included wisdom, victory and wealth. Always the ally of Zeus, she was greatly respected on Olympus, although it did not appear to be her lot to dwell there. One legend tells of how she incurred Hera's wrath by stealing her make-up to give to Europa. In fleeing to Earth to escape the punishment of the mother of the gods, Hecate sought shelter in the house of a mortal woman who had just given birth to a child, a contact which rendered Hecate impure. So that her pristine state could be restored, the Cabeiri escorted her to Acheron and henceforth she became a divinity of the Underworld. As Prytania, queen of the dead, her area of magic included purifications, expiations, enchantments and magical charms. All hauntings, both pleasant and unpleasant, were attributed to her and her minions, her most frequent visitations apparently taking place at crossroads, near burial places, or the scenes of crimes. Triple-faced figures of the goddess were therefore frequently found at crossroads and these were inevitably honoured on the eve of the full Moon. The crossroad retained its sinister reputation for many centuries, the bodies of suicides or violent criminals being buried there in the hope that Hecate would find them quickly and despatch them hastily to her domains, thus removing any possible nuisance factor they might constitute for the locals nearby. She was accompanied on these nocturnal wanderings by a retinue of infernal hounds.

Persephone

The story of Persephone, or Kore, having already been told, all that remains for discussion at this juncture is the etymology of her name and her specially designated area of magical activity. The name Persephone can be broken down into two halves, the first of which means 'to destroy' while the latter stems from the root word 'to show' — 'she who destroys the light'. Another interpretation given is 'dazzling brilliance'. Not being originally an infernal deity, Persephone therefore partakes of the flavour of both kingdoms — Olympus and the Underworld — which brings us back to Demeter and the Eleusinian connection. The Mysteries would appear to be telling us that in order to partake of the bright light of wisdom we must also come to know and conquer the darker regions, both of the astral underworld and our own self.

Persephone's attributes were the bat, narcissus and, for obvious reasons, the pomegranate. She was seldom invoked as a divinity in her own right on account of her close association with her mother, Demeter, the Mysteries of Eleusis being shared equally between the two goddesses. Her magical energies are, therefore, encapsulated in that Mystery cult and all that it implies.

Divinities with Olympian Associations

Dionysus

Semele, daughter of King Cadmus of Thebes, caught the amorous eye of Zeus and a love affair ensued. Hera, however, eternally jealous of her husband's infidelities, disguised herself as a nurse and slyly suggested to Semele that she request her lover to appear to her as he really was, for how else could she be sure that he was not, in fact, some fearful monster! Realizing the destructive effect such a manifestation would have on Semele, Zeus begged her not to ask such a favour, but Semele was adamant and the father of the gods was compromised into a position where, in order to keep his word, he was obliged to display his full radiance. Being unable to endure such dazzling fire, Semele was immediately consumed and the child she carried in her womb would also have perished were it not for a thick shoot of ivy which miraculously created a green screen between the unborn babe and the celestial fire of Zeus. Gathering up the infant, Zeus enclosed it in his own thigh; when its time was come he drew it forth with the aid of Ilythia and so Dionysus was born.

The myths tell us that Zeus made several more attempts to shield Dionysus from Hera's wrath, episodes during which those who aided his efforts were severely punished by Hera, usually by being driven mad. Upon his reaching manhood Hera bestowed a similar fate on poor Dionysus, who consequently spent the ensuing few years roaming the world in the company of his tutor, Silenus, and a wild band of satyrs and maenads. The staff which he carried was ivy-twined and tipped with a pine cone; called a 'thyrsus', this is a powerful symbol in Greek magic as we shall see.

After many more years of wandering, plunder, madness, destruction and suffering, Dionysus was finally established as divine and welcomed into Olympus by his father, Zeus, the gentle Hestia standing down to give him her seat.

Although there are many interpretations of the Dionysian legend, notably Robert Graves' suggestion that it refers to the spread of the vine cult across Europe, Asia and North Africa and its accompanying side-effects, the whole story can also be submitted for occult or metaphysical analysis, where it assumes a far more interesting significance. Although the later association between Orphism and Dionysiac rites will be dealt with in Chapter 7, there is one cogent point worthy of comment at this juncture: Dionysus basically represents mankind. His madness, destructive tendencies, drunkenness and hedonism were all negative traits which he was obliged to overcome before he could attain to godhood. In other words, during the process of experiencing and conquering his weaknesses he was, like each and every one of us, a god in the making. Born of a union between mortal woman and the divine fire, he lived through the madness of destructive misunderstanding and the blindness of inebriated folly, slowly ridding himself of those shackles through a process of gradual self-development and eventual mind control. An understanding and knowledge of his tutor, the satyr Silenus, is one of the deeper mysteries of Olympian magic, as we shall see.

Pan

It is generally agreed that Hermes was the father of Pan, but his mother is sometimes mentioned as being either Dryope, the nymph Oeneis, or Penelope, wife of Odysseus. The more convincing story, however, is that this benign Arcadian deity was the product of a union between Hermes and the goat Amaltheia, or even the son of Cronus and Rhea.

The Olympians, it seems, exploited Pan. Apollo wheedled the art of prophecy from him and Hermes copied a pipe he had left lying about, claimed it as his own invention and promptly sold it to Apollo. In spite of his 'divinity', the story was told that news of Pan's death came to a sailor named Thamus. A spirit voice supposedly instructed the mariner to proclaim, upon reaching Palodes, that the great god Pan was dead!

But what Thamus, who was an Egyptian, probably repeated was the ceremonial lament, 'The all-great god Tammuz is dead!', which he could have misheard somewhere on his travels. During Plutarch's time, in the latter half of the first century AD, the old god was apparently very much alive, shrines, altars and caves dedicated to him being regularly frequented.

Occultly, Pan is highly significant. In addition to his magical syrinx there is the famous 'Pan call', the notes of which will be dealt with and explained in Part Two.

Themis

We have already considered Themis's relationship with Zeus and the high regard he held for her counsel. Another story tells how she made Apollo a present of the oracle at Delphi which she had inherited from her mother, Gaea.

Themis was a goddess of justice. Her epithet *soteira* suggests a protection of the just and punishing of the wicked. As a wisdom goddess she was known as Euboulos, the good counsellor. Her task on Olympus also involved maintaining good order, regulating ceremonial events and presiding over public assemblies.

Helios and Selene

Although the Greeks considered Apollo to be the god of the solar light, the orb of the Sun itself was accorded a separate divinity, Helios. The cult of Helios probably originated in a much earlier pantheon that pre-dated the Olympians by many centuries. Helios drove a chariot that was drawn by a team of magnificent white winged horses whose names were Lampon, Phaeton, Chronos, Aethon, Astrope, Bronte, Pyroeis, Eous and Phlegon.

Just as Helios guided the chariot of the Sun across the heavens from east to west so, as her brother retired, Selene commenced her lunar journey across the night sky. Her vehicle was not always a chariot, however, as she was sometimes shown mounted on a horse or mule.

Occultly, Helios and Selene represent the 'lights' in astrology, their influences relating to natural forces rather than specific archetypes. Although nine names are given for the steeds of Helios, he is traditionally shown in a chariot drawn by only four horses representing, no doubt, the quarternary principle. The number '9' has additional significance: as the last single number it is associated with Martian or physical energy while, according to Hermes Trismegistus, the horse represents purified passion, the implication being that the personal energies need to be mastered (reined in) if the solar power is to be harnessed successfully. Selene also connects with the number '9' through the Qabalistic Sephirah, Yesod the Foundation, which in spite of its lunar or passive connotations has a masculine or active aspect.

Dione

Originally a Pelasgian divinity, Dione was the daughter of Oceanus and Tethys and, according to some sources, the mother of Aphrodite by Zeus. Her close association with Zeus may be evidenced in the functioning of the Dodona oracle, her priestesses apparently sharing the oracular gifts equally with the priests of Zeus.

Ilythia

There were two Ilythias at one period, both daughters of Hera, who presided over birth and brought relief to women in pain with labour. No child could be born unless they were present and no mother could find relief from her pains without them. Although Artemis was later worshipped as goddess of childbirth, on account of her own miraculous birth, she did not appear to interfere with these two minor goddesses in any way. Later, Ilythia became a single divinity, but the truth is that her archetype had probably been carried down from pre-Hellenistic times and could be traced back to Minoa and earlier. Ilythia is usually depicted kneeling, with a torch in one hand and the other hand extended in a gesture of encouragement.

Iris

A personification of the rainbow, Iris was the sister of the Harpies and one of the Olympian messengers. In her divine form she appeared clothed in a long tunic, her hair was held by a bandeau and she carried a caduceus. Golden wings were attached to her shoulders and, like Hermes, she was often depicted wearing winged sandals.

Although she mainly served Zeus, Iris was devoted to Hera; in addition to carrying her messages, she also effected the goddess's vengeance. She was obviously a caring sort of deity for the myths tell us how she welcomed the other gods on their return to Olympus, unharnessed the steeds from their chariots and brought them nectar and ambrosia. The fact that she is shown in such a benevolent light conveys the message that life's storms are often followed by a rainbow, from which illumination we may receive solace, good news and hope.

Hebe and Ganymede

Hebe was worshipped by the Greeks as a goddess of youth since she personified the beautiful young maiden who never aged. The duties of divine cup-bearer were hers until she incurred Hera's wrath over some minor incident, when she was replaced by Ganymede. But the mother of the gods finally repented and, when Hercules was eventually admitted to the Olympian company, she gave him Hebe to wife.

Ganymede was venerated at Sicyon and Phlius conjointly with Hebe. He is depicted as a beautiful adolescent youth in a Phrygian cap and was sometimes carried through the air on the back of an eagle. Zeus was particularly struck with Ganymede's beauty and arranged for him to assume the role of his personal cup-bearer.

The magical lesson to be learned from these two godlings is that while beauty of form and face might, at certain stages in our development, appear to aid our ascent up the spiritual ladder, they can also chain us to a life of service. And, although the being whose cup we bear may assume divine aspects in our eyes, this particular role must eventually be relinquished if the aspiring Hero is to stand alone and be his own person in the cosmic scheme of things.

Zagreus

Before her uncle Hades whisked her off to the Underworld, Persephone gave birth to Zeus's son, Zagreus. The Curetes of Crete, or maybe it was the Korybantes who guarded his cradle, but whoever was responsible fell foul of Zeus's old enemies, the Titans, who came under disguise by night and stole the infant. In his attempt to escape from their clutches, Zagreus changed form many times, becoming Zeus in a goat-skin, Cronus as the raingiver, a lion, a horse, a horned serpent, a tiger and a bull. At the final point the Titans seized him by the horns and hastily despatched him. Athene happened to witness the dreadful deed and, noticing that Zagreus's heart was still intact, enclosed it in a gypsum figure into which she breathed life so that he became immortal.

Zagreus's later association or possible identification with Dionysus is no doubt a throw-back to the violent rites that were common to both godlings prior to the civilizing influence of the philosophers.

To do justice to the nature and personality of all the minor deities would reach well beyond the scope of this publication. The aforegoing, therefore, is rendered purely as a general guideline or starting point from which the dedicated student of the Heroic Path may step forth into his own line of study and investigation.

5. NON-HUMANS, FABULOUS BEASTS AND NATURE DIVINITIES

There were, believe it or not, times in the history of man when he *was* aware of the existence of other life-forms, energies or minds equally as powerful and intelligent as his own, if not more so! Prior to the onset of his spiritual blindness, man paid due deference to the denizens of other dimensions and the energies that ensouled river and stream, forest and cave, wind and fire. In the myths, names are accorded both to the group elemental soul and to those spirits that individuated from it, a few examples of which are given here. However, we are only skirting the edges of this study so there is considerably more to be learned by those with the time, inclination and dedication necessary for its pursuit.

The Satyrs

Said by some authorities to represent elementary spirits of the forests and mountains, satyrs were but one of many groups of beings which were partly of human and partly of animal form. They are described as having low foreheads, snub noses, pointed ears and hairy bodies, goats' tails and cloven hooves. According to Graves, the most famous of these was Silenus, whose name means 'Moon man'. Larousse, however, designates the *Sileni* as a whole and separate species, being originally genii of springs and rivers, in which case they would have more in common with the mythological 'water horses' than the satyr genus. As our own 'inner planes' teaching accords with Graves' interpretation, for the purpose of this book we will leave Silenus in satyr form.

Silenus was traditionally considered to be a loud, jovial, permanently drunken sort of lout, who also possessed a never-ending source of knowledge and innate wisdom which he saw fit to dispense on certain occasions, notably his encounter with King Midas when he expounded the Atlantis story in some detail. As tutor to Dionysus, Silenus accompanied his charge during the wild, mad days of the godling's initiations. Plato, however, felt no irreverence in comparing his master Socrates with Silenus, so what is the answer, and why should an ugly, drunken old half-man, half-beast hold so much magical sway?

Of course, as with all Greek magic, there is an inner mystery involved. Satyrs, centaurs, sileni, unicorns or winged horses may form part of a muddled unreality to some people, in much the same way that pink elephants are jokingly associated with the state of inebriation but, in another dimension or parallel universe that co-exists simultaneously with and within our own, they are realities! Man may accidentally peer into this universe when seriously ill, in his 'cups', or under the influence of hallucinogenic drugs because, on such occasions, the discarding of programmed conditioning allows the barriers to drop sufficiently for the veil to be temporarily drawn aside. But to the Initiate of the Heroic Path these universes are available for viewing *at will*, the spiritual development of the viewer being the only deciding factor as to the nature and intensity of the revelation. To the uninitiated soul Silenus and his ilk may well appear as hedonistic inebriates, because satyrs and centaurs are of the nature of Pan in that they act as mirrors in which man may confront himself! Once the heroic Initiate has learned to break from the 'collective' and programme his own mind without resorting to *stimulants of any kind*, he will see the satyrs and their friends as they really are and come to know himself into the bargain. The godling within him will have started to stir in its gestation and the satyrs, centaurs and their associates, being fully aware of their tutorial role, will step forward to help him on his way.

The fact that the Greek heroes were usually born of a god to a mortal mother is in itself an indication that the god force was already sufficiently manifest within them to bring about the essential individuation which is a 'must' for every occult initiate.

The Centaurs

Forming part of the cortège of Dionysus, the centaurs had the torso and head of a man while the remainder of their body was of a horse. Etymologically, the name centaur signifies 'those who round up bulls' (Larousse, *Encyclopedia of Mythology*), which makes our equestrian friends sound like a group of mythological cowboys! But, like their satyr friends, the centaurs were also renowned for their wisdom. It was said that Chiron, in particular, was educated by Artemis and Apollo and he, in turn, passed his knowledge on to many of the heroes. When wounded by Hercules Chiron exchanged his immortality for the mortality of Prometheus, a sacrifice for which Zeus placed him among the stars as the constellation of Sagittarius.

In earlier chapters we considered the nature and deeds of Prometheus, the Titan, and his specific role in the evolution of mankind. Chiron's noble gesture, therefore, tells us that the inhabitants of that parallel universe, which our mortal eyes are as yet unable to behold, have entered a temporary state of transition (death) in order to allow Prometheus to finish the task he commenced with his gift of fire. When man has learned to master the divine fire within his soul, then will the world of Chiron be once more open to the scrutiny of all. Until such golden times, however, the privilege is reserved for those whose heroic deeds of self-discipline, love and universal understanding earn them the right to learn from Chiron and his contemporaries.

Pegasus

When the gorgon Medusa was decapitated by Persus, the children she was carrying by Poseidon — Chrysaor the warrior, and Pegasus the winged horse — sprang from her dead body. Both had been conceived, rather irreverently, in the temple of the goddess Athene, which apparently caused that divine personage considerable offence.

The mortal Bellerophon, son of Glaucus, was asked to destroy the Chimaera, a fire-breathing she-monster. Before setting out on this mission he consulted the seer, Polyeidus, who advised him that the success of his mission depended on his catching and taming the fabled Pegasus. Bellerophon sought the beast and found him drinking from a pool. Using a golden bridle which Athene had conveniently presented to him, he was able to catch Pegasus, mount him and set off. So successful was the team of man and winged horse that Bellerophon's services as a hero were much sought after by mortals and immortals alike. One day, however, he overstepped the mark by presumptuously undertaking a flight to Olympus on the back of Pegasus. Zeus, being affronted by such conceit, sent a gadfly which stung Pegasus under the tail, causing him to rear and send his rider tumbling back to Earth. Pegasus completed the journey to Olympus, where he was greeted by Zeus and the other gods.

Although the ancient Egyptians are, perhaps, better known for viewing the immortals in forms other than those of *Homo sapiens*, the Greeks were just as much believers in the occult fact that divinity can assume any form, as may be evidenced in this Pegasus story. Bellerophon, for all his heroism, had not yet attained to godhood, but Pegasus the horse was welcomed into the divine company. A lesson in humility for man, perhaps? For the Initiate, *definitely*.

An interesting point to note: Aquarius, whose energies rule the New Age, falls under the constellation of Pegasus. Perhaps, during the Aquarian Age, we are destined to witness the uniting of man with some of the more misunderstood or rejected facets of existence outside his own environment, together with a spiritual acceptance of those animals that dwell with him on his own planet.

Not all the fabulous beasts were as gentle and evolved as Pegasus, however. There were an equal number of 'nasties' to be contended with. These were usually seen as conglomerations of whatever the Greeks of those times saw as being ugly or horrendous. It is not difficult to sort the wheat from the chaff; a little logic does the trick, so one does not need to be all that mysterious about it. Many of the 'creatures of evil' which the heroes were sent forth to dispose of represent aspects of the 'self' which need to be faced up to and conquered. But more of this when we set about analysing the Labours of Hercules in a later chapter.

The Muses

As god of music, Apollo was always accompanied by a group

of supernaturals known as the Muses. These varied in number, the original three being Melete, Mneme and Aoide, while the names of Nete, Mese and Hypate were given to them at Sicyon. In Lesbos seven Muses were acknowledged, while the Pythagoreans favoured eight of them. Nine were finally chosen: Clio, Euterpe, Thalia, Melpomene, Terpsichore, Erato, Polyhymnia, Urania and Calliope. Each has a specific function as follows:

Clio: Muse of history. Her symbols were the heroic trumpet and clepsydra.

Euterpe: Patroness of the flute, this being her symbol.

Thalia: Originally a bucolic Muse, she later became patroness of comedy. She is depicted carrying the shepherds' staff and comic mask.

Melpomene: The Muse of tragedy. She carried the tragic mask and the club of Hercules.

Terpsichore: Mistress of lyric poetry and the dance. The cithara was her attribute.

Erato: Muse of love poetry.

Polyhymnia: Originally Muse of heroic hymns, she was later designated Muse of mimic art and shown in a meditative pose with her finger on her mouth.

Urania: As Muse of astronomy Urania has as her attributes the celestial globe and compass.

Calliope: The senior of the nine Muses was honoured as muse of epic poetry and eloquence, her symbols being the stylus and tablets.

The Horae

The name Horae signifies a period of time which can be applied to the year, season or hour. The Horae were meteorological divinities who showered the earth with rain, without which nothing could grow. Later they were said to preside over nature itself and the order of the seasons, but there was considerable confusion as to their true roles even in those distant times. They varied in number, with the people of Athens favouring Thallo, the bringer of flowers and Carpo who brought fruit, while Hesiod counted three: Eunomia, Dike and Irene (or Eirene); Eunomia saw that laws were observed, Dike watched over justice, and Irene ensured a state of peace. On Olympus they had special tasks, one of which included guarding the gates of heaven. Eunomia, Dike and Irene were the daughters of Zeus and Themis. They were shown as beautiful maidens with flowing hair, golden diadems and light footsteps. They loved to dance and often accompanied the Graces to form part of Aphrodite's retinue. They were also the helpers of children and young people generally, to whom they showed much tenderness and care.

The Moerae or Fates

Homer saw these beings as representing man's individual and inescapable destiny; it was only Hesiod who treated them as minor divinities. Daughters of Night, they were three in number and were named Clotho, Lachesis and Atropos. Clotho, the spinner, personified the thread of life; Lachesis, chance, the kindly element of good luck that we all hope will appear at some propitious time in our life, while Atropos stood for those fatalistic conditions that are generally designated as being karmic from which we would appear to have no escape. The Moerae shadow the whole of a person's life. They arrive with Ilythia at the moment of birth and are present at the point of death when it is their duty to sever the cord. In ancient Greece they were also invoked at the time of marriage to ensure a happy and lasting union.

The Keres

When it was destined that a person should meet with a difficult or violent end, this onerous task was executed by the Keres, who were sometimes called the 'Dogs of Hades'. This rather unpleasant group of spectres apparently did the dirty work for the Moerae, but they were not alone in this task, being assisted by the Erinnyes.

The Erinnyes

Also known by some as the 'Dogs of Hades', this little chthonic band were entrusted with the special mission of punishing the crime of parricide and the violation of oaths and promises. No doubt many of the aforementioned were purely personifications of moral ideas or principles, as was Nemesis, for example, and the serious student should have no difficulty in sorting one from another.

Cerberus

Guardian of the gates to Hades' Underworld, Cerberus was a mighty watchdog with fifty heads and a voice of bronze. His parents were Typhoeus and Echidna. Sometimes he was depicted with only three heads but bristling with serpents. Either way, he was a pretty terrifying sort of character and once inside his gates there was little chance of escape.

The Underworld was surrounded by the river Styx and in order to cross this, or any of the subterranean waterways, one needed the help of the old ferryman, Charon. Unless the deceased presented Charon with his *obolus* he could not hope for his assistance, which meant being stranded in a sort of no man's land between life and death. Then there was the river Lethe, which flowed to the extremity of the Elysian Fields on the one hand and to the edge of Tartarus on the other. Those who drank its waters forgot all that had previously transpired in much the same way that many people are born with no memory of former lives or experiences.

The Sirens

Coming from the Greek root meaning 'to bind or attach', the name Siren gives us a clear indication as to the role of these beings in the make up of the human psychology. They were originally depicted with the legs of a bird and the head of a woman and, as with all feathered or winged beasts, they stood for the negotiation of the next dimension as well as this Earth. Later the bird aspect gave way to the fish's tail and we find ourselves with traditional mermaids of the sort that perch on rocks and comb their hair, supposedly luring seamen to their doom.

Occultly, we are dealing here with emotional principles (as with all associations with the Element of Water), the bird, or higher aspect, giving way to the feeling and flowing instincts which, as we all know, can be a trap in themselves if one is not careful. The Sirens were not all bad, however. They were skilled musicians, especially with the flute and lyre, and possessed singing voices of great beauty.

The Nereids

Fifty daughters were born to Nereus the truthful and Doris, daughter of Oceanus. They were fair-haired and beautiful and dwelt with their father beneath the ocean. Nereid sisters often made mythological news: Thetis, for example, who features so strongly in the Zeus story, and Galatea whose escapade with Acis has been the inspiration for poetry and music down the ages.

The Nymphs

We have already seen how the Meliae or ash nymphs were born from the spilled blood of Uranus but the term 'nymph' in Greek mythology is employed to cover a whole range of devas and not simply the Ondines or water spirits so well known to modern occultists.

Nymphs were beautiful, youthful and charming. They inhabited the rivers and streams and kept watch in the forests and on the mountains. The Greeks gave them different names according to the region with which they were associated. The Oreads were the spirits of mountains and grottos; the Napaeae, the Auloniads, the Hylaeorae and the Alsaeids haunted the woods and valleys, while the Dryads were the forest or tree spirits. The Hamadryads were so closely associated with trees that they probably represent entities of the tree or vegetable evolutionary strain and not actual elemental protectors.

The Four Winds

Eos, the dawn, and Astraeus, the starry sky, had four sons: Boreas, the north wind; Zephyrus, the west wind; Eurus, the east wind; and Notus, the south wind. The Element of Air features in several classical legends and is usually personified in one or other of these four winds which are obviously manifestations of the quaternary principle.

The Harpies

The Harpies also had air associations, but of a less pleasant nature. They represented storms and tempests and usually brought ill luck or hardship as a result of their pranks. In later times they were shown as hags, although this was not the way in which they were originally portrayed. Natural forces, like any other form of pure energy, can appear constructive or destructive and the Greeks, in their vividly pictorial personifications, drew a very clear dividing line between the two aspects.

The Sphinx

Unlike the benign Egyptian Sphinx, the Greek version was anything but friendly. She was the daughter of Typhon and Echidne and sported a woman's head, lion's body, serpent's tail and eagle's wings. Sent by Hera to punish Thebes for displeasing the goddess, she settled on Mount Phicium, near to the city, and asked everyone who passed by the answer to a riddle she had learned from the three Muses: 'What being, with only one voice, has sometimes two feet, sometimes three, sometimes four, and is weakest when it has the most?' Anyone unable to render the correct answer was immediately despatched and devoured by her.

One day Oedipus chanced along that road and, guessing the answer, made the reply: 'Man, because he crawls on all fours as an infant, stands firmly on his two feet in his youth, and leans upon a staff in his old age.' Completely shattered by her defeat the Sphinx threw herself from Mount Phicium and was dashed to pieces in the valley below, whereupon Oedipus was acclaimed king. The message here would appear to be that once man has recognized his weaknesses and strengths, he is then ready to despatch the evils of blind ignorance which have previously condemned him to captivity or death.

* * *

As an acknowledgement of and good relationship with the elemental and nature forces is essential to the aspiring occultist, so he or she who chooses to tread the Heroic Path must also observe these courtesies. But such observations must be born of love and respect rather than knowledge and fear. So, whether you choose to employ the ancient Greek names for these energies or discover new individuations for yourself from among their ranks is essentially a personal thing. And, after all, the Heroic Path is tailored for the individual!

6. THE ELEUSINIA

The cult of the 'Mystery' was very much a part of early Greek life, the necessity for its existence being accepted at all levels. During his many years as a practising psychiatrist and psychoanalyst, Carl Jung observed the innate need in man to acknowledge and respect a force or beingness more exalted or powerful than himself. Whether this force is personalized monotheistically or polytheistically is of little consequence; it is through the mental effort of reaching beyond himself that man gains the impetus to negotiate the next stage in his evolutionary progression, an action which also helps to effect a balance between his transpersonal and conscious self.

There is considerable speculation regarding the real Eleusinia. So closely were its secrets guarded that Athenian law punished by death anyone who tried to probe them either out of sheer curiosity, a sense of rebellion, or simply as an ego trip. Down the ages various scholars have tried to piece the picture together from fragments of writings by early Christian doctors, stalwart adherents to the pagan cults, and scholarly historians. But as far as is generally known the Mysteries of Eleusis were said to have originated somewhere around 1800 BC and provided the Greeks with a mystical system equal to anything the Egyptians had to offer at the time. However, its magical elements would appear to differ considerably from those of Egyptiana and, as we are dealing mostly with hearsay, any serious comparison is out of order.

In his book *The Mysteries of Eleusis* (Aquarian Press), Goblet D'Alviella mentions certain characteristics which all the Mystery schools shared. These he lists as:

1. The fulfilment of preparatory or purifying formalities which brought the profane to a state of readiness to receive the initiation.

2. Transfer of 'sacred objects' (Παράδοις των ἱερων). These ἱερά were sometimes formulas taught orally (Λεγομενα, Συνθηματα) and sometimes symbolic objects which were put on exhibition or were handled by the neophyte (Δεικύμενα, Δρώμενα).

3. Performance of mythological legends, either by priests or by the neophytes themselves.

4. The absolute prohibition of revealing to the profane the actions or words which formed the secrets (τὰ ἀποῤῥητα) of the initiation.

When the Mysteries were at their height, three grades were involved: the Small Mysteries, the Great Mysteries and Epoptism. Every respectable citizen of Athens endeavoured to become initiated at the higher or more secret levels, but there was also a public side in which glorious pageantry and outward display served to keep the man in the street happy. The priestly or inner ceremonies were administered by two families: the Eumolpides and the Kerykes, whose offices extended throughout the whole period of early paganism until the eventual triumph of Christianity.

Obviously, one had to pass through the Lesser Mysteries before the doors to the inner *sanctum sanctorum* were opened. These were celebrated towards the end of winter, in the month of *anthesterion*, just after the flower festivals or Anthesteria which were sacred to Demeter and Dionysus. The Great Mysteries were celebrated in September in the month of *boedromion*, between the time of harvesting the grain and sowing the new seeds. However, there was often a repeat of the Lesser Mysteries held at the end of summer to spare the beginners, many of whom had travelled from afar to witness the rites and become initiated into them, a second and perhaps costly journey.

The Small or Lesser Mysteries were also known as the Mysteries of Agra as they were celebrated in Agra, a suburb of Athens, and not Eleusis. Anyone could attend these, it appears, even foreigners. Among the scant fragments of archaeological information available is a painted vase which shows the divinities involved in the ceremony. Demeter is seated in the centre with the traditional calathus head-dress; Aphrodite is at her right hand and Eros at her feet. On the left is Persephone, torch in hand, and the young Iaccus holding the cornucopia. Also present were Dionysus, complete with magical thyrsus, and Hercules armed with a club. The officiating priest and those undertaking the initiatory rites were also in evidence.

The Great Mysteries commenced on the thirteenth day of *boedromion* when the young men left for Eleusis to fetch certain sacred objects which were then placed in the care of the high priest. On the fifteenth day of the month there was a general gathering of the neophytes of both sexes, which did not always end in an orderly or spiritual manner, the servants of the Baccanalia making sure of that. The sixteenth day saw the mystics setting out for the seashore, each bringing a sacrificial piglet to offer to Demeter, with men and piglets together entering the waves for purification.

The seventeenth day involved floral tributes to Dionysus and a wake in honour of Asclepios who, like Persephone and Dionysus, had also spent a period in the Underworld. Day eighteen saw everyone assembling to carry the statues of the goddesses to the temple of Asclepios for the Epidaurean celebrations.

On the nineteenth day the procession assembled in front of the Eleusinion (at one period it was the Pompeion). A statue of the young god Iaccus, crowned with myrtle and holding a torch, was borne ahead. Iaccus would appear to be no more than the personification of some local tutelary spirit, who was granted the right to serve Demeter and later became fused with Dionysus the child. Various fetishes were also carried, each object holding a deeply mystical or magical significance. The remaining first fruits of the harvest, supplied by the general populace, were placed in pots and carried on the heads of the Kernophores, or white-robed priestesses. Four white horses carried the tall calathus basket containing the sheaves of corn.

The long procession covered some twenty kilometres leaving Athens via the Dipylon gate. All along the way there were chapels, shrines and short stays for rest and worship.

And, of course, the usual gathering of fortune-tellers, artists, purveyors of magical paraphernalia, and the inevitable ladies of easy virtue. For those interested in the finer details of the proceedings Goblet D'Alviella supplies them in his aforementioned book.

Needless to say, the final stages ended in a giant orgy with everyone over-imbibing, so it is little wonder that the satyrs and their friends also appeared in this light. When the necessity for public celebrations of an orgiastic nature come up for discussion, we are reminded of the dialogues between Anebo, priest of Anubis, and Porphyry. That these revelries relieved public tension was one explanation, the inference being that the ordinary people were presented with an opportunity to work something out of their system, after which the streets were safer for gentler folk to walk during the ensuing weeks.

On the twentieth day the neophytes engaged in solemn sacrifice to the gods. From then until day twenty-three there would appear to be a degree of conjecture as to what actually took place, but it is generally agreed that at some point the story of Demeter must have been enacted accompanied by some form of ecstatic meditation which was guaranteed to put the neophytes in touch with those who dwelt either in Hades or the Elysian Fields.

Epoptism was considered the highest and most secret initiation to be undergone. Plutarch assures us that one could not hope to penetrate such Mysteries until late in life, but there were no doubt exceptions.

There is much disagreement among historians and scholars regarding the days of these final ceremonies and what actually took place. But, from a study of the aforegoing, it might seem logical to assume that the twenty-fourth and twenty-fifth were days of importance. All we do know is that those initiates who passed their tests received a medal inscribed with the head of Demeter, an ear of corn, a poppy and the word ἔποψ, several of which have been discovered in the Eleusis area.

As with most systems of ceremonial magic, drama also featured strongly in the initiatory rites, with the stories of Demeter, Persephone and those other divinities who had at some time paid a visit to the regions of Hades playing a prominent part. In the *Thesmophoria*, which was celebrated in Attica in the month of October, the absence and return of

Persephone was dramatically commemorated, although it is generally agreed that the public Eleusinian rites were by no means confined to the enactment of this legend.

Although ancient Greek magic featured a degree of role-playing ritual, which it no doubt inherited from earlier times, after the onset of the cult of the Hero a gradual transformation took place with logic assuming the reins that had previously been held by intuitive promptings and the need for overt devotional expression. In other words, that very Aquarian thing — individual responsibility — experienced its birth throes in the heroic deeds of the classics.

In his book *Fragments of a Faith Forgotten* the Theosophical scholar G. R. S. Mead insists that the open state Eleusinia, with its processions and public participation, was tainted at the inner levels by the disorderly elements of undisciplined oriental cults that had fused with it over the years, while its outer show was purely political. The real Mysteries, we are informed, belonged to the Orphic tradition.

7. ORPHISM AND THE LESSER RITES

Homer's celebrated hymn to Demeter makes no mention of Dionysus among the Eleusinian gods, which rather suggests that his cult probably started independently and was incorporated into the Lesser Eleusinia at a later date. Its origins are obscure, although it is generally agreed that it carries oriental overtones. Mead opines that it contains both Chaldean elements and archaic Semitism, and that the god was not of Thracian origins as is generally believed.

Tales of Dionysus's riotous exploits in the company of a ribald band of nymphs, satyrs and maenads are hardly suggestive of spiritual sublimities, but then the people of those early times no doubt visualized the god in their own image and likeness as is, sad to say, ever the case with man!

The vine being sacred to Dionysus, the bulk of his followers, as with the Phrygian Sabazius, considered drunkenness to mean divine possession. In later more civilized times devotees likened the plucking, crushing and pressing of the grape to form a pleasing nectar to the progress of the soul which is formed whole and then crushed and pressed into shape by the trials of its earthly adventures, eventually to re-emerge as a refined and useful intelligence. This analogy was seen in the life of Dionysus himself, whose purification through the way of madness and suffering finally gained him admittance to the Olympian band.

In spite of the aforegoing, there is a certain 'prodigal son' quality about Dionysus which hints at an inner teaching. Could the suggestion be, perhaps, that no matter to what depths of degradation our wayward steps may take us, there is always the light of knowledge and love to lead us back onto the straight and narrow path of return to our Father on high?

In the process of his redemption Dionysus suffered deeply, but then that is surely the price paid by anyone who abandons himself to pure hedonism, the ascent from the resulting abyss constituting a much harder climb than that endured by the meeker, more stolid person who has strayed little from the Father's side. And yet, if we are to heed the words of the parable, it would appear that because the experiences undergone by the prodigal son were fuller and more comprehensive than those encountered by his more cautious brother, the rewards were correspondingly greater. Divest this story of its materialistic connotations and we are left with something a little nearer the truth, which is probably that both contribute equally to the 'whole', all experiences being necessary to 'its' expansion.

The original Dionysian Mysteries were apparently concerned with the re-enactment of the god's hapless adventures and eventual period of suffering. This naturally established the mode of abandonment for which certain earlier aspects of the cult became famous. But with the advent of the Pythagorean schools a new, more spiritual quality slowly crept in.

Amidst the orgies, sacrifices and riotously overt 'devotionalism' that dominated the Eleusinia, the balance was maintained by the emergence of small communities of men and women who gave themselves entirely to holy and disciplined living. These were known as Orphics. When Pythagoras established his famous school at Crotona, he did little more than refuel an existing tradition that had survived the centuries in spite of the negative Dionysian traits that pervaded the more popular or public Mysteries. Mead tells us the Pythagorean schools were absorbed into Orphism. Plato continued the work of the master, but added to it the dimension of reason so that the truth behind the Mysteries could be more easily assimilated and its benefits made more readily available to the uninitiated.

At some stage the Cretan god Zagreus became closely associated with Dionysus, almost to the point of mergence, but according to other sources he assumed a Siva-like role as the great hunter, or god of death, while Dionysus, in his capacity as god of life and rebirth, guaranteed delivery and salvation. To the suffering, passion and resurrection of Dionysus, the adepts of Orphism added a new mysticism and the character of the god underwent a profound modification. Out of the window went the wine, orgies, hedonism and delirium and instead there emerged — in the words of Plutarch — 'the god who is destroyed, who disappears, who relinquishes life and then is born again'. In other words, Dionysus became, like the Egyptian Osiris, the 'risen one'.

It would seem logical to assume that the Orphic Mysteries were initiated by someone of that nomenclature, in which case a consideration of the nature and legend of Orpheus is called for, if only to supply further clues as to the origin of the cult.

Orpheus was a hero of Thrace, but unlike the regular crop of Greek strong men he was not known for his exploits at arms. Being a son of Apollo he had inherited his father's musical talents to such a degree that when he sang and played the lyre even the most savage of beasts would lie gently before him. This talent he put to great use during his adventures with the Argonauts on their quest for the Golden Fleece. So powerful, in fact, was his music that even the denizens of the Underworld fell under its spell.

Orpheus was married to the nymph Eurydice, whom he loved above all else. But one day, when fleeing from Aristaeus, his wife received a mortal wound from a serpent. So heartbroken was the bard that he made it his business to descend into the infernal regions where he charmed Hades and Persephone sufficiently for them to allow Eurydice to be returned to him. The one condition was that at no point on the return journey from death to life should he turn to look at his beloved.

Eurydice, being naturally delighted to see her husband once again, begged him to turn his face towards her. When he failed to comply with her wishes she took this as a mark of rejection and informed Orpheus that unless he made this obvious gesture to reassure her of his continued affection she would assume that his love had died, in which case she would prefer to stay with Hades. Being greatly moved by her impassioned plea Orpheus turned to her, which act cost him his love for ever. This kind of single-minded devotion was not understood by the Thracian women of the time and legend has it that they tore him to pieces in their anger, casting his head and lyre into the river Hebrus. Later the head was seen to be caught between some rocks where, for a long time, it delivered oracles. There are many other legends concerning the ultimate fate of Orpheus, but who he was and what happened if he really existed is open to conjecture.

Taking this story into account, the fact that the Orphic cults carried strong musical connotations is hardly surprising. At first glance, Orpheus and Dionysus would appear to be strange bedfellows — almost opposites — the one representing the faithful lover and gentle musician whose power lies in his manipulation of harmonious sounds; while the other, as god of wine and abandonment, appears initially in a less favourable light. Surely the Mysteries are telling us that although wine may loosen the mental barriers between the material and etheric worlds sufficiently for us to become aware of their existence, if we are to negotiate them successfully it must be via the path of suffering that we will eventually gain sufficient mastery of the 'self' to secure us a safe passage through altered states of consciousness, without the need for recourse to the fermented juice of the grape. Orpheus, on the other hand, shows us an alternative way through beauty, art, gentleness and fidelity. Yet, in spite of his basic goodness, he had to descend to Hades and suffer the loss of that which he loved the most. Dionysus is surely the god within us trying to manifest against the weaknesses of the flesh, external environmental programming and overwhelming material odds, while Orpheus represents our more gentle traits which we may develop if we feel so inclined. Perhaps there are two distinct paths open to us, neither being either right or wrong.

Orphic ritual, naturally, consisted of a mixture of the attributes of both Orpheus and Dionysus. From the Orphic influence there was music, while the unbridled rites of earlier Dionysiac cults gave way to the disciplined movements of the ritual dance. Do the Orphic rites have a place in today's occult world? This is a matter for individual choice, of course, and the only advice we would proffer is that if they are treated with the discipline and respect that Pythagoras accorded them, then well and good. There are elements in modern society that need little encouragement for hedonism, with its inevitable toll on health and its negative role in the welfare of the community at large. If you wish to pursue the Orphic line, consider the nature of the hero who gave his name to it and learn from him. Then tackle Dionysus, but only after Silenus has accepted you as a pupil; and therein lies the Mystery!

In addition to the better known Eleusinian, Dionysiac and Orphic paths, there were many subsidiary systems of mystery and initiation some of which probably never made the historical records, not to mention the myriad undesirable elements that masqueraded under mystical-cum-magical banners. Mead refers to the Thiasi, Erani and Orgeones and hints at several other oriental cults which later emerged in Mithraic references. However, the modern student of Greek magic need not concern himself too much with the somewhat suspect historical trivia surrounding these earlier cults; better that he discover his own personal path of initiation which is more suited to today's world.

8. THE ORACLES

If we are to subject oracular divination to a close scrutiny we must first consider the nature of time itself. Our present concepts of linear time are already being questioned in scientific circles and, although the alternatives may prove somewhat difficult for the conditioned mind to compute, they would appear to be nearer to the truth than many might imagine.

The aspirant to the Heroic Path is advised to consider his spiritual 'self' in terms of a shattered hologram, the fragments of which exist simultaneously through the stationary bands we shall refer to as 'time zones', each zone offering a unique experience to the evolving soul. Therefore, once the veil which isolates any one segment from the other has been penetrated, the student has at his command a reference to any time frame — past, present or future. In other words, when we have overcome our programming sufficiently to look beyond the limiting confines of our present existence, we will have access to whatever records we need, when we need them. Not that this knowledge precludes us from the ordinary mêlée of living — far from it — but it can furnish us with the weapons necessary to deal with our adversaries, be they aspects of ourselves or obstacles laid across our path by others. Remember, the aspiring Hero is always given the weapons which the gods deem necessary for each task and, if he uses them wisely, there is no reason why his efforts should not meet with success.

There would appear to be a subconscious yearning in man to reach out to his other fragments, a purpose for which he may choose to court the good offices of those intermediaries he designates as being able to assist him in this quest. Over the centuries these have appeared under different labels: angels, guides, spirits, gods, saints, spacemen, the 'collective unconscious' and even what are felt to be 'past lives'. Of course, we are by no means the first to recognize this factor. In his treatise, *De Divinatione*, Cicero states:

> It is an ancient belief, going back to heroic times but since confirmed by the unanimous opinion of the Roman people and of every other nation, that there exists within mankind an undeniable faculty of divination. The Greeks called it *mantike*, that is the capacity to foresee, to know future events, a sublime and salutary act that raises human nature more nearly to the level of divine power. In this respect, as in many others, we have improved upon the Greeks by giving this faculty a name derived from the word god, *divinatio*, whereas according to Plato's explanation the Greek word comes from *furor* (*mania* from which *mantike* is derived). What cannot be gainsaid is that there is no nation, whether the most learned and enlightened or the most grossly barbarous, that does not believe that the future can be revealed and does not recognize in certain people the power of foretelling it.

From the aforegoing we may gather that it is the futuristic aspects of divination that are the most popular and easily accepted; after all, we are already familiar with what has taken place in the past. But the reference here is to the past and future of our present life, or what the fates have in store for us in our particular 'neck of the universal woods' at this juncture in time, whereas the broader concept of non-linear time opens up far too many doors for comfort — or so many might feel. It was Emerson who commented to the effect that God offers to every man the choice between truth and repose; we may take which we will but we cannot have both! Now, perhaps, the need for the aspiring Hero's valour is becoming more obvious.

The most famous of all Greek oracles was undoubtedly that of Apollo at Delphi. We have already established that this spot was not always sacred to Apollo, he having inherited it from previous divinities, notably Earth herself, which surely suggests some sort of power centre or emphatic point in the energy circuits of the planet at which it is easier to make contact with other universes or time zones, probably because the 'veil' is thin.

The site of Delphi lies in Phocis, in the centre of Greece, some two thousand feet above the waters of the Gulf of Corinth. Leaving all mystical considerations aside, the sheer beauty of the environment must have spoken to the hearts of the men and women who paid fealty to its lords. Apollo's oracle was presided over by a priestess known as the Pythia, who always took great care to acknowledge all local and former deities whose servants might previously have occupied the prophetic chair.

The Delphic oracle was by no means limited to fortune telling. According to Euripides, Earth 'conjured up dreams and nocturnal visions which laid bare the past, the present and the future to countless mortals as they slept'. Earth's gift of oneiromancy does, however, give us a clue to the knowledge and nature of a people who might conceivably have known more about the intuitive nature of man than their more logical Greek successors.

In those earlier times there was a resident sibyl at Delphi who, we are told, frequently entered the trance state often employing the gift of tongues. Likewise, her Apollonine successor, the Pythia, was, from descriptions reported, often out of her body when her famous prophetic utterances were made. Even that archetypal seer, Cassandra, was said to become greatly perturbed during certain altered states of consciousness, which all goes to suggest that prophetic ecstasy was very much favoured in those times, possibly because it was deemed to be more impressive than less dramatic time-probing techniques.

The ensuing passages from the pen of Diodorus Siculus, however, throw further light on the subject:

> In ancient times it was the two goats who first discovered the oracle, which is why in our day the people of Delphi still prefer a goat when they offer sacrifice before a consultation. The discovery is said to have come about in the following manner. At the spot where the *adyton* of the present temple is there was once a chasm in the ground, where before Delphi was yet a city the goats used to graze. Whenever one of them approached this

> chasm and looked down into it, she would begin leaping about in an amazing fashion and bleating in a quite different voice to her normal one. And when the shepherd, marvelling at this prodigious behaviour, examined the chasm to find out what caused it, he himself was affected in the same way as the goats, who in truth behaved for all the world like people possessed, and began to prophesy the future. Later, news of what happened to those who visited the chasm began to spread among the peasants, and they flocked to the spot in large numbers, anxious to put the miracle to the test; and whenever one of them drew near he fell into a trance. Thus it was that the place itself came to be regarded as miraculous, and they believed that the oracle came to them from Gê, the Earth goddess. For a time, those who came thither to seek advice used to proclaim oracles to one another. But, later on, when many people in their ecstasy had hurled themselves into the chasm and disappeared, it seemed good to those who lived in those parts that, for the protection of others, one woman should be appointed as the sole prophetess, who alone should pronounce the oracles. They therefore constructed a device so that she could sit in safety when the spirit entered her and utter her oracles to those who sought advice from her. This device was supported by three legs, hence its name, tripod; and indeed the bronze tripods that we have today resemble it almost exactly.

It would therefore appear that a vapour (*pneuma*) originally issued from the earth at that point. This induced a state of semi-consciousness which allowed easy access to the subconscious or transpersonal 'self' on the one hand, or to any external intelligence with a message to render on the other.

Apparently, Apollo was not always at the beck and call of everyone at his famous shrine as he took a regular winter vacation. During his absence Dionysus took over, but according to records both cults existed happily side by side. Plutarch, himself a priest of Apollo, remarked that 'as regards the Delphic oracle the part played by Dionysus was no less than Apollo's'.

For a long period the Pythia only pronounced formal oracles from the *adyton* once a year on Apollo's birthday, the seventh day of Bysios, or the beginning of spring. This later became extended to include every seventh day of the summer months, Apollo being the seventh god and '7' his sacred number. However, it was possible to obtain a private reading for a fee, known as the *pelanos*. These fees could take any form from sacrifices to the gods to private pay-offs. Plutarch provides us with some considerable detail concerning the *modus operandi* of the system which unfortunately space does not permit us to recount.

In earlier times, the Pythia was always a young girl or virgin, after the style of Apollo's sister, Artemis. But following an incident when an enquirer took advantage of the beautiful young maiden in office and carried her off, it was decreed that the prophetess should, henceforth, be a lady of fifty years or over. Writing of the Pythia in the first century AD, Plutarch says:

> The woman who at present occupies the position belongs to one of the soundest and most respected families to be found in Delphi and has always led an irreproachable life, although, having been brought up in the home of poor peasants, when she fulfils her prophetic role she does so quite artlessly and without any special knowledge or talent. Like the young wife Xenophon describes in his *Oeconomica*, who should know nothing of the world when she enters her husband's house, the Pythia is almost completely ignorant and inexperienced, so that when she approaches the gods she does so with a truly virgin heart.

Many people today share the view that intellectuals do not make good mediums as they have a tendency to 'monitor' the messages with logic, which sometimes alters the meaning. And yet there is always the problem of communicating entities who wish to impart information of a more scientific or scholarly nature being limited by the education or vocabulary of their vehicle. So it is probably a question of personal preference on the part of the communicating entity.

Although the site of the Delphic oracle is known, it would seem that archaeologists have not been successful in locating the original sanctuary. There is considerable conjecture as to who removed all the traces and why. Perhaps the pagans were instructed by Apollo to close the doors or encapsulate the energies until such times as the god was ready to resume his dialogues. Or maybe it was the Christians who carried out the process of obliteration. Nor is there any geological evidence for the existence of those trance-inducing fumes, although it is not beyond the realms of possibility that movements in the earth's sub-soil could have caused the original orifice to close up. Although there have been quite a few guesses made as to how the whole Delphic scene was stage-managed, nobody knows for sure and an air of mystery persists; but the accuracy of its utterances have been sung by poet, philosopher, scholar and historian, which leaves us in no historical doubt as to its existence.

The difference between Cassandra the sibyl and the classical Pythia are worth a comment. Whereas the priestess's gift would appear to have been used only when sitting upon the sacred tripod in the Delphic locale, Cassandra's seership was always with her, no matter where she went. Can we not read into this yet another indication that the power of the mind should not be limited to ritual or environment, but allowed to function freely at any place or time?

Delphi was by no means the only oracle of repute in ancient Greece. Zeus's oracle at Dodona also has its claim to fame. The Pelasgians, ancestors of the Greeks, believed that the voice of Zeus could be heard whispering as the wind stirred the oak trees. Zeus's companion at this oracle was the Earth goddess, later identified as Dione, whose priestesses shared responsibility for its functioning with the representatives of the father of the gods. The oak was certainly sacred to Zeus and there was no doubt that one tree in particular was favoured for oracular purposes. Bronze bowls were also employed at this site, the sounds they emitted as the wind moved them being interpreted by the attendants. Clients could also inscribe their questions on sheets of lead which were then handed to the attendant priests or priestesses. One or two of the answers that archeology has unearthed show how the people of those long departed times were as much concerned with the trivialities of their lives as are the many folk who consult psychics today for advice as to how to deal with annoying neighbours, succeed in their businesses or find their true calling in life. Cleromancy (divination by lot) is also referred to by Cicero as being connected with Dodona and, as the thunderbolt was Zeus's sacred weapon, all forms of atmospheric phenomena — *meteora* — acquired considerable significance.

The oracle of Trophonius, at Lebedea in Boeotia, had a flavour all of its own. Trophonius, it seems, was a local nature divinity who failed to find a place among the gods but was allotted a heroic role. He had a grotto for his oracle with an opening just wide enough for a man to squeeze through.

The whole process of entry was, it appears, somewhat daunting as it involved a difficult descent to the *adyton* under conditions guaranteed to instil fear into all but the bravest hearts. When the clients finally emerged they were usually in pretty bad shape physically and, although they were often quite confused by the event that had taken place, they were sufficiently aware of the advice given to be able to record it on a tablet for the priests in charge, just to make sure they had it right!

In Lybia the oasis of Ammon apparently sported an oracle which was greatly revered by Alexander the Great. It is described by Diodorus Siculus as 'covered with emeralds and other jewels' and its deliveries involved overt religious ceremonies which were designed to stir the emotions and render the clients open to suggestion. Music, dance and ritual were employed to achieve the necessary ends.

There were many smaller and less significant oracles dotted all over the Greek empire. Many of these were Apollonine in nature, while others maintained the strict order of resident sibyls which had been passed down since the time of the matriarchal system. There were also many famous seers who functioned outside the oracular sanctuaries. Cassandra we have already mentioned, but Calchas, Amphiaraos, Tiresias and Megistias also spring to mind.

Messages spoken by seers, sibyls and oracles were seldom initially explicit, clients often being sent away mystified, the truth only dawning on them when some major occurrence in their life served to clarify the situation. But, overall, it seems that people were happy with what they received.

The Greeks employed many systems of divination in addition to the recognized oracles. The behaviour of birds, fish, animals and natural phenomena was carefully observed and translated into prophetic terms. But then these methods and signs are as valid to many people today as they were in those distant times. So-called 'old wives' tales' differ little from the superstitions of days past, many of which are now being re-examined in the light of new knowledge encountered by the extending frontiers of science and psychology.

The subject of Greek oracles is worthy of a study unto itself and students of magic wishing to fill in the finer details are recommended to the book *Greek Oracles* by Robert Flaceliere (Paul Elek Ltd, St. Albans, 1965).

9. MAGICAL SYMBOLISM BEHIND THE HEROIC ADVENTURES

The classical ethos has exerted such a profound influence on the world's thinking that its allegory is still effectively employed in today's world to convey ideas and emphasize ideals. What then is its secret? Is it, as Graves and other classical scholars would have us believe, purely an intellectualized folk record of history and customs long past which serve to enlighten us regarding the horrendous deeds of our human ancestors? Are there, as others maintain, cosmological references contained in the fables which speak of vast epochs of time beyond the scale of our imagination? Does it embody a folk memory of an earlier more scientific culture, such as Silenus's Atlantis, which has been translated into magical terms of reference for want of a better explanation? Or is it a mixture of all these, concealed amongst which are certain basic cosmic truths?

If asked for a decision we would prefer the latter, in which case, in order to substantiate our inclinations and opinions, we must provide some justification for them. Since the occult does not function on a frequency that man has yet invented the technology to measure, any esoteric teaching must of necessity be open to conjecture and/or adjustment in the light of the continuing stream of new information from both the scientific and metaphysical disciplines. But, taking into account what we feel guided to state at this juncture, there would appear to be some profound cosmic truths which are blatantly evident in the old Greek beliefs and their accompanying legends.

Under parapsychological investigation the heroic adventures yield some interesting data; apply basic occult principles to the formula and a decidedly logical, enlightening and informative pattern emerges. To cover the esoteric significance of every heroic deed would take many volumes and years of work, but in the second or practical part of this book we will embark upon the task of examining the twelve Labours of Hercules in the initiatory light, the revelations of which, we trust, will spur seekers of the Heroic Path to apply the principles employed to the many other deeds and misdeeds so beautifully illustrated in the classics.

What we are dealing with is a series of parables which describe the basic nature of man and his *raison d'être*, as far as this planet is concerned. Interwoven throughout this whole fabric is an unbroken thread which carries clear instructions as to how to rise above the whole scene and ascend to loftier realms. But, first of all, the monsters within us — the Ids, or shadowy aspects of the personality — must be taken to task and despatched.

Legend has it that many, if not all, famous persons from the past, who have left the kind of indelible marks upon our planet that have aided its progress towards the light of justice, reason and love, were born of some strange union between the immortal and the mortal. Alexander the Great believed himself to have been born of a divine father to an earthly mother, and even the British bard himself is said to have been a fairy foundling raised by mortal parents. Fairy, magical or immortal origins suggest a link with the infinite which can raise the person in question above the rank and file of ordinary folk; and yet this does not necessarily imply a ready access to the high spiritual places.

What, then, are we being told? Surely, that there comes a time for each and every one of us when the god-spark within us becomes sufficiently activated to propel us into the kind of spiritual forward motion necessary for our first step on the ascent up the danger-strewn paths to the Olympian heights! At this point we elect to enter a body which carries a certain genetic code, one, perhaps, that has been handed down by the gods or devas who first spawned life in this terrestrial place. The knowledge of our divine cosmic roots is, therefore, locked safely within our genes to surface as and when our interests and studies serve to activate it. Like a sealed time capsule, it holds its information securely and secretly until the correct code is issued, whereupon in true computer fashion it feeds its program, little by little, to the conscious mind for practical enactment. Once this activation has taken place, the prospective Hero finds him or herself impelled to proceed towards the arduous task of spiritual ascent. Fall and fall again as he or she will, the upright posture will eventually be resumed and the wounds healed as the gods will always be standing by to aid their own progeny on their homeward journey from the terrestrial wastelands. Along that road the aspiring Hero will encounter every kind of obstacle, delay and deception, plus a goodly sprinkling of malign fabulous monsters, some of them purely aspects of himself that need to be expunged before, like Dionysus, he may take his place in his father's house.

Many who read the aforegoing will wonder why all the emphasis is placed upon the aspiring Hero. What about the ordinary people who have no heroic aspirations? Have the gods forgotten them? This book is primarily about Greek magic and the journey of the soul along the Heroic Path. Each of us may, in any given time zone, assume that heroic role, but this present time may not be the right one for us. However, the lesson learned from an understanding of the theme may well serve to unlock the doors of understanding for us in some other time zone or, to use the more popular linear explanation, in a future life. No knowledge is ever wasted. The mind is like a computer; it can store the facts and lessons of experience and draw upon them at a touch of the right mental button. People are often surprised at the genius of prodigies, and teachers appear nonplussed when one or two pupils in their class appear to have knowledge which is out of keeping with or far in excess of their years. Dare we suggest that in some other time zone they are possibly reading this book, or others like it that the servants of truth have seen fit to record for posterity?

10. THE ESOTERIC SIGNIFICANCE OF OLYMPUS

Most beliefs carry a concept of some exalted or heavenly regions to which the just, or those committed to an acceptance of the designated divinities, are entitled to enter upon completing the round or rounds of their earthly existence. Heavenly states fall into several categories, some more mystical or esoteric than others.

Unlike the Christian heaven, Olympus was not a place where those who had been 'good' during their earthly life merited a comfortable existence on a diet of nectar and ambrosia. The gods had a right to dwell there because of who they were, having achieved their immortality in some timeless age or environment unfamiliar to the limited spiritual concepts of men.

During the Homeric period or earlier, the popular Greek view was that upon leaving the body at the moment of death the soul of the average person shed much of its earthly personality and assumed a vague, ill-defined and somewhat insubstantial quality. Those who had left some mark of distinction while on Earth were allowed to retain their individual characteristics in Hades, however, a doctrine which is probably re-echoed in the modern Spiritualist belief that deceased doctors, teachers and other learned people continue to carry out their work in the afterworld.

For the Greeks the only hell, as such, was Tartarus, as distinct from the Underworld or realms of Hades. Tartarus was reserved for the outstandingly evil or those who had committed crimes against the gods themselves (broken cosmic law?) and its inhabitants were probably tortured more by their own guilt than by some personalized demon. Surrounded by a triple wall and the waters of Phlegethon, its best known prisoners included the Titans, Tityus, Tantalus, Sisyphus, Ixion and the Danaids, all of whom had been condemned to some form of personal physical discomfort.

Elysium, on the other hand, could be equated with the Spiritualist concept of the 'Summerland' — a place where the Sun always shone, soft refreshing breezes caressed those who dwelt therein and all was beauty and repose. In earlier times it was believed that Elysium was reserved for the children of the gods, but later it was declared open to those who had found favour with the Olympians, and to the souls of all just men.

Slowly the idea evolved that Hades' Underworld was a place in which each received his just desserts according to what he had merited during his life on Earth. Upon arrival there the soul was required to appear before a tribunal composed of Hades and his three assessors: Aeacus, Minos and Rhadamanthys. After judgment had been pronounced the soul was either cast into Tartarus, or conducted to the Elysian Fields or the Islands of the Blessed.

But these were not the only beliefs by far. The philosophers as far back as Heraclitus considered the soul to be part of the universe itself. Upon death the body fell to dust and was reunited with the Earth, but the spark which had animated it ascended to some higher place. In a series of lectures given by Franz Cumont, which were later incorporated into a book entitled *Astrology and Religion Among the Greeks and Romans*, we read:

> The official epitaph of the Athenians who fell at Potidaea in 432 BC, expresses the conviction that the ether has received into its bosom the souls of those heroes as the earth has received their bodies.

The Orphics and Pythagoreans gave credence to the idea that the souls of the departed withdrew to the Moon, or some star or planet, while Plato's view was that souls that have made good use of their lives return to inhabit the heavenly bodies from which they originated prior to their birth here on Earth. Now this is an interesting philosophy in view of current esoteric credos that favour the existence of 'star people' among us, meaning souls who had previously evolved in other parts of the universe.

It was a long held doctrine in Greek tradition that fabled heroes were rewarded for their exploits by having their names immortalized among the stars: Hercules, Perseus, Andromeda and the Dioscuri, for example, so it would appear that what we are faced with when considering the Greek attitude towards the hereafter is a variety of opinions influenced by the individual depth of understanding, or school of philosophy adhered to. While most of the ordinary people probably accepted the Elysian/Hades concept, the thinkers or more enlightened minds rejected this as illogical, along with the annihilation belief that was also accorded credence by some, and sought deeper explanations.

What, then, was Olympus all about if there was no chance of entry on merit? Logic demands that at some point the created have a right to return to the Creator, and therein lies the esoteric significance of the Olympian ideal.

Mount Olympus rises to some nine thousand feet above a steeply flanked plateau. Its sheer slopes are clothed with dark woods, tumbling torrents and deep folds. The line of the peak assumes the appearance of an amphitheatre, the upper tiers of rock appearing as giant throne-like seats. Nature itself enters the conspiracy by causing moving wisps of mist to assume supernatural shapes amidst the stunning beauty of the general panorama. So it is little wonder that the primitive peoples of those parts saw in this wild and mystical terrain a suitable dwelling place for the gods. We are, therefore, dealing with two aspects of Olympus: (1) the exoteric, or 'image and likeness of man', which views the gods as wreathed in the mists of the Mount itself, from which vantage point they lord it over the faithful below, while at the same time participating fully in the whole gamut of mortal virtues and vices; and (2) the inner or esoteric concept, which calls for elucidation.

Olympus is obviously not a place of rest, replenishment and reunion with loved ones, where one receives a nice pat on the back for being good. It represents a state of beingness that each individual soul or spirit from *all* regions of creation may return to become re-absorbed into, once it has rediscovered and developed the god-force within it. We are all gods in the making, and we will achieve the Olympian heights *only* when we have overcome our mortality or conquered death through the Path of Initiation. Mortality means eventual death; the immortal do not die. In other words, they have risen above that state whereby it is necessary to reincarnate into matter in order to learn and experience. The Greeks no doubt inherited this idea from an earlier and more spiritually knowledgeable race, but the concept degenerated as human foibles and weaknesses were superimposed upon the gods to the extent that their original meanings became lost or obscured.

And so we are left with the classical heritage, with its tales of immortals, heroes, monsters and elementals, originally calculated, perhaps, to show a race of young souls the sort of difficulties they were likely to encounter on the road home to the gods. A few of the heroes of old achieved this immortality, notably Hercules, so it could be done. But for the time being the rest of us were deposited in some Elysian Summerland, a Hades of forgetfulness, or the purgatory of Tartarus.

No. Greek magic does *not* deny any individual the right to ascend to Olympus, in fact it clearly points out the path. It is then up to those who would assume the Heroic Role to seek their tutelary deity, their symbols of individuality (the god symbol and personal symbol: see *Practical Techniques of Psychic Self-Defence*) and bravely set out on the hazardous upward ascent. The aspiring Hero may on his journey encounter monsters like the Sphinx, the Gorgon or Typhoeus. He may be driven temporarily insane, meaning that for a short period he loses his ethical sense of direction and is unable to accept responsibility for his own actions. But this state does not last for ever and, when the benign divinities see that he has endured enough, the helping hand is inevitably extended.

This principle was beautifully illustrated in a modern motion picture, *Jason and the Argonauts*, in which the gods were shown playing a game of chess, with the heroes as the pieces. As each piece was moved into a position on the board which equated with an adversity on Earth, so the tutelary deity countered with another move which righted the situation.

Does this mean, therefore, that we are like puppets in the hands of the gods and must dance at their beck and call; and who are these gods anyway? In the first place nobody forces us to seek the aid of any external force or energy. We do so by our own free will. Admittedly, this free will may function more actively prior to entering an incarnation, so that we are rather like a train in that once we have been placed on a particular track we tend to proceed along the lines ahead; the most we can do to effect a drastic change of direction is to ask someone to change the points for us, or get out and do it for ourselves. But nobody compels us either way, nor are we forced to take on any particular incarnation. What would appear to occur is that the adventurous soul, anxious to prove itself and make good progress in a particular life, may bite off more than it can chew. Sometimes, when questioned under hypnosis, a person who is going through a particularly bad patch of difficulties which he consciously resents will inform his therapist that he is delighted with the way things are going as the goals he set out to achieve are now in sight! So we are faced with a veritable 'Janus' as far as free will is concerned: the conscious or everyday side, which would appear to be making the decisions on the surface, and the transpersonal side which often holds opposing views. When these two aspects come into conflict a neurosis or psychosis takes over and, as with those heroes who offend the gods, a form of madness, breakdown, or temporary insanity ensues. In fact, it is the god aspect within the 'self' that has induced the alienation and not Zeus, Athene, Hera or any exterior influence.

Regarding the true nature of the gods themselves, let us put it this way: the universe is held together as a cohesive whole by an intelligent force or group energy. Every living creature is imbued with a unit of this energy, which endows it with life as we know and understand it. Being intelligently motivated, these energies can individuate into principles or 'frequencies' known to past civilizations as 'the gods'. A much earlier spiritually and scientifically advanced race, maybe from Atlantis, perhaps from outer space, whose existence has frequently been hinted at throughout this book, possessed a set of symbolic keys for use of and contact with these frequencies. Sadly, many of these degenerated into pure superstition, while a few survived in fragmented and incoherent form to surface within a series of abstract disciplines later to become designated 'the occult'. The nomenclature ascribed to these energies or principles were legion, and oft-times borrowed from those teachers who originally instructed man in their doctrines. As time went by the names of famous rulers, healers, mystics, nature divinities and local godlings were added, obscuring the original sonic vibrations to such a degree as to render them totally unrecognizable.

But is this really so? Perhaps, deep within the genetic coding of the potential Hero, there lies the knowledge of the true names of the gods. The Egyptian goddess Isis, mistress of magic, was said to have gained her powers from Ra by tricking the old god into revealing his name to her, upon receipt of which knowledge she immediately became all-wise! The clue, therefore, lies in that spark of the godhead within us or, to use the Greek magical idiom, our immortal heritage.

11. THE PHILOSOPHERS, ASTROLOGY AND GREEK LOGIC

Franz Cumont tells us that all sidereal cults were originally quite foreign to the Greeks which, he feels, goes to prove that their common ancestors hailed from the north where the constellations were frequently obscured by the weather. Although the Sun and Moon were regarded as divinities they occupied a secondary place in the Greek religion, other principles appearing more dominant. Aristophanes pointed out that the basic religious difference between the Greek and surrounding pagan cultures lay in the fact that the former favoured personal deities such as Hermes or Athene, Greek logic being opposed to the deification of celestial bodies devoid of human feeling, while the latter worshipped the Sun and Moon as they appeared in the heavens.

Naturalistic beliefs were never really extinct, however, as may be evidenced in the Pythagorean doctrine which expresses the divinity of the heavenly bodies as being motivated by a superior universal soul, akin to the nature of the spark which gives life to man. Plato accused Anaxagoras of atheism, because the latter dared to suggest that the Sun was merely a gaseous mass and the Moon an Earth-like structure. To Plato the planets and stars were visible manifestations of the gods or superior energies from which stuff the universe came into being.

Astrology in the form we now know and recognize probably seeped into Greece from Chaldean or Babylonian sources. When the Greeks first learned of the five planets known to antiquity they gave them names according to their character. Venus was called 'herald of dawn', 'herald of light', or 'vespertime'; Mercury, the 'twinkling star'; Mars, the 'fiery star'; Jupiter, the 'luminous star'; and Saturn, the 'brilliant star'. After the fourth century BC the planets were known by the names of Hermes, Aphrodite, Ares, Zeus and Cronus, probably because the Babylonians dedicated them to Nebo, Ishtar, Nergal, Marduk and Ninib respectively, the gods in one system equating with their counterparts in the other.

One of the earliest recorded Greek astrologers was Thales (639–546 BC). He was reputed to have studied in Egypt, but left no written evidence of his teachings or philosophies. He is famed for having predicted an eclipse that caused much alarm and ended the battle between the Medes and Lydians, the date of which was fixed by the seventh Astronomer Royal in 1835 as being 28 May 585 BC.

Pythagoras, Anaxagoras, Plato and Eudoxes all studied astrology in Egypt, as did Hippocrates, who used it extensively in medical diagnosis. The philosophers varied in their views as to the motion of the Earth in relation to the Sun, Moon and planets, Aristotle, for example, believing that the Earth was fixed in the centre of the universe.

According to Margaret Hone's *The Modern Text Book of Astrology* (p. 289), it was Hipparchus (190–120 BC) who was regarded as the founder of observational astronomy.

> He measured the obliquity of the ecliptic. Making use of Chaldean eclipses, he was able to evaluate the Moon's mean motion. In 134 BC he discovered a new star. He then set to work to catalogue all stars to know if any other new ones appeared. In so doing and comparing with earlier lists, he found that all stars had changed their places with reference to that point in the heavens where the ecliptic is 90 degrees from the poles of the Earth, i.e. the equinox. He found this could only be explained by a motion of the equinox in the direction of the apparent diurnal motion of the stars. This was the discovery of the *precession of the equinoxes* and was necessary for the progress of accurate astronomical observations.

Here we have a splendid example of the application of Greek logic to an occult art, thus effecting a marriage between physics and metaphysics. Astronomy and astrology were one!

Posidonius of Apamea (135 BC), a Syrian, was also learned in astrology and founded a school in Rhodes which was visited by Pompey and Cicero. His doctrines were said to have inspired the *Astronimica* of Manilius. Claudius Ptolemy (AD 100–178) wrote the *Almagest* and the *Tetrabiblos*, both of which exerted a profound influence upon later schools of astrological thought.

Having examined the historical evidence for the rise of astrology in ancient Greece, is it possible to relate the beliefs of these early scholars to the modern study and application of the art? Did the Olympian pantheon correspond with the planets or signs of the Zodiac?

The one clue we have is contained in the work of Gaius Manilius (48 BC–20 AD), who wrote:

> Pallas rules the woolly Ram and Venus guards the Bull,
> Apollo has the handsome Twins and Mercury the Crab.
> Jove, with the Mother of the Gods, himself is Leo's lord.
> The Virgin with her ear of corn to Ceres falls, the Scales
> To Vulcan's smithy, while to Mars the warlike Scorpion cleaves.
> The Hunter's human part Diana rules, but what's of horse
> Is ruled by Vesta with the straitened stars of Capricorn.
> Aquarius is Juno's sign as opposite to Jove,
> And Neptune owns the pair of Fish that in the heavens move.

As may be clearly seen, the god natures of the old pantheon do not appear at first glance to equate with modern astrological interpretations. Or do they? Take a closer look and you will be surprised at what you see. Athene ruling Aries, for example, which leaves the broody Mars to cope with the hidden passions of Scorpio. Not so very illogical after all! There are many more clues in Manilius's lines for the aspiring Hero to unravel and here is how to go about it:

First, make a careful study of the nature of each god, and his or her associated zodiacal sign. It will not be long before it becomes clear to you that the Greek god-forms contact an occult aspect of the zodiac that evades detection at first glance. When choosing your tutelary deity bear these correspondences in mind, for you will find yourself carrying out certain important heroic tasks at the time when your tutelary divinity's corresponding sign is accentuated either by eclipse, lunation or planetary emphasis.

Of course, astrology was not the only magical art that was logicized in the Age of Reason. The numerological system labelled 'Pythagorean' is still in use today and favoured by many as against the more complicated Chaldean method.

The orthodox modern-day student of the classics might well enquire as to how great minds such as Plato and Pythagoras, with their strictly logical approach to philosophy, reacted to a world of magical fantasy and supernatural powers. The answer must obviously be: 'Not with the same incredulity that their modern counterparts see fit to employ.' Or dare one suggest that there are no such counterparts in our present day and age because, if there were, they would appraise the occult facts in much the same way as did the logicians of old.

12. THE EGYPTIAN AND OTHER EXTERNAL INFLUENCES

The wisdom of the Greek philosophical giants did not suddenly emerge, but was the result of a slow accumulation of knowledge over the centuries. Pythagoras, for example, was preceded by Pherecydes, Anaximander and Thales in Asia Minor, while the Chaldean and Babylonian influences on Greek astrology and the oriental hegemony within the Mysteries have already been the subject of comment.

In the time of Thales, who lived a century earlier than Pythagoras, the educated and travelled Greeks looked to Egypt for learning and culture rather than to their own forebears. Only the ignorant and superstitious, Mead tells us, believed in the old barbaric ways, and thinking men were obliged to seek outside their own environment for spiritual or philosophical enlightenment. At the end of the sixth century BC, however, there was a new interest aroused in the old legends, led by one Onomacritus. With the recovery of her own lost identity Greece was able to flex her political muscles and assume a stronger position in the civilized world of the time. This period coincided with the revival of the Orphic tradition and the increased activity in the general religious life of Greece. Old horrendous tales were translated in a new and more spiritual light; Greece had found her true self at last!

There were, however, many external ingredients in the Greek recipe, some of which had been added to the melting pot many thousands of years earlier. In his *Critias and*

Timoeus, Plato has preserved for us the story from the records of the priests of Saïs which they had communicated to Solon. It tells of how, as long ago as ten thousand years earlier, Attica had been occupied by the ancestors of the Hellenes. But a great flood came that destroyed Atlantis and rocked the Mediterranean shores with seismic disturbances that finally brought about the Flood of Ducalion. During this period of disturbances the 'Pelasgi', as Herodotus calls them, were subjected to an influx of immigrants from both the north and south, many of which must have been Atlanteans who had either already been resident in the land, or survived the Flood by fleeing there during the period of high danger. The religious admixture that emerged must, therefore, have been a hotch-potch of Atlantean tradition, goddess worship and primitive animism which was eventually to become submerged beneath the oncoming tide of conquering Aryan patrism.

But nothing is ever lost. It may lie dormant for long periods, but eventually it will surface and make its mark when the time is right. With the advent of the philosophers and the accompanying regeneration of past beliefs, many old, pre-Flood teachings must have seeped through amidst the wild tales of monsters, revengeful gods and orgiastic rites, and it is the thread of these truths, slim though it may be, that provides the basis for true Greek magic as practised by the pursuant of the Heroic Path.

Every ethos has the right to disclose the truth according to its own unique design — and this does not mean *distort* it! How any of us feel as regards the occult disciplines of the past will be coloured by the culture, or time zone, in which we first imbibed the deeper esoteric knowledge. Many of you who read this book will be able to relate to the Mystery schools of classical Greece, or maybe to even earlier Hellenistic or Pelasgian times. These stirrings will serve to activate the genetic memory code and slowly, surely, the first recollections of immortal parenthood will start to dawn. The gateway to the upwinding path of immortality will have been opened . . . and you, the aspiring Hero, will be ready to commence your ascent to freedom . . .

PART TWO
THE PRACTICE

13. TUTELAGE AND TUTORAGE

There are many ways of approaching the practical magical path. With some systems it is simply a question of finding others who are compatible both personally and occultly and setting up a joint study group, or seeking the help of qualified persons who have themselves studied under recognized and fully proven teachers or masters. There is an abundance of occult literature available on the more popular traditions and several reputable societies and groups only too happy to steer the serious and dedicated student in the right direction.

But with Greek magic we are dealing with an entirely different set of rules. Remember, the Heroic Path is the lone path, ideally suited for the man or woman who does not wish to embark on the group experience, so the methods already mentioned are not really applicable. Neither has much been written on the subject, from which the student may glean information and knowledge or benefit from the first hand experiences of others. Where and how, then, does one start?

First of all, let us examine the question of suitable reading matter. Books dealing with the Olympian system may be few and far between, but there are the classics which have been well-documented throughout the ages. The aspiring Hero need seek no further than a good book on Greek mythology as his or her starting point. But care should be taken not to place too much credence on explanations and interpretations provided by historians and experts, ebbing and flowing trends in philosophy, psychology, archaeology and religion having inevitably influenced scholarship over the years. Keep an open mind and see how *you* feel impressed to interpret the stories. Follow the classics with some of the more detailed works referred to in this book, by which time you will have formed a firm opinion as to your own chosen path of ascent to the Olympian heights. But in addition to all this there is what for the aspiring Hero must be the most important step in his or her initiation: acquiring a tutelary deity and attracting a tutor.

The path of the aspiring Hero, being a lone one, he or she who would venture along it may not turn to another human for assistance. Olympian magic is not of the role-playing variety, nor does it provide a seat in an institutionalized classroom. Every aspiring Hero must place him or herself under the protection of one of the twelve Olympians. Without this tutelage there can be no journey, as there will be no commencement. The first initiation, therefore, comes in the selection of the correct god or goddess.

It may seem odd to many that one needs actually to 'choose' a divine guide in this way. But not so for the aspiring Hero who is subconsciously, if not consciously, aware of his divine origins and is, therefore, only reaching back to his 'parent'. There is a humorous saying that 'it is a wise child that knows its own father'. Never did this apply more than in heroic magic. And yet that immortal relative might well be a goddess; after all, did not Athene, Artemis, Hera and the other goddesses aid many a hero?

Of course, choosing your tutelary deity is not a decision to be taken lightly and a lot of deep consideration, meditation and study should precede the final decision. It is rather a question of 'Man, know thyself', because in knowing oneself and realizing just what and who one is one will become aware of one's spiritual ancestry or cosmic roots.

Let us move on a stage further. The god or goddess having been chosen, some form of confirmation or acceptance will be given. This will occur in a perfectly natural way. It may be experienced through a dream in which a location, a statue or an actual visitation from the deity features prominently. Or, during the normal course of a conversation, someone may unconsciously make a confirmatory suggestion; or, perhaps, a book will be opened at just the right page. But, would-be

Hero, remember it is between you and the god, so you cannot go running to a medium for corroboration if you are unsure. Just wait until the 'all clear' is given to you from Olympus, as it surely will be.

In an ensuing chapter details of the twelve Olympians will be given to serve as a general guide. You must select one of them as 'family' and principal protector and, although minor deities may be invoked for specific purposes, a sense of security and trust must be built up between you the would-be Hero and the Olympian deity of your choice.

If one cannot seek instruction from another man or woman who then, you may ask, is there to turn to, and from whom does one obtain one's esoteric information? The myths supply you with this knowledge if you read them carefully. Closely interwoven with our own universe (so close in fact that one actually functions within the other) is another, for want of a better term, 'parallel' universe, wherein dwell many forms of life totally dissimilar to our own. To the denizens of this realm their world is real and solid; because it functions at a much faster frequency than the carbon structures of Earth, it passes through our world in the same way that X-rays, gamma rays and neutrinos pass through our bodies.

This invisible universe is one of many such dimensions which may accidentally be encountered by those whose programming has been temporarily suspended by the use of certain drugs, the over-imbibement of alcohol, serious illness or mental disorders in which the conscious mind has lost the power of rationalization. But the strange fact is that the human brain does contain the facility for its recognition and negotiation by *conscious* control, and therein lies yet another Herculean task for the aspiring Hero. Psychically gifted folk whose minds are not closed to the concept of other intelligent life forms may be able to catch a glimpse of these unseen realms, however, and as the familiarity grows a full and comprehensive perception eventually becomes possible.

Within this parallel universe dwell those creatures who represent a meeting or uniting point between many types of creation. A sort of evolutionary melting pot, if you like. As any occultist worth his or her salt knows, the gods are not in man's image and likeness, nor are they in the image and likeness of any other evolutionary strain which may have evolved in the infinity of time and space. Each race of beings tends to fashion its deities as it sees itself and all but the wise will accept this generalization. Man is not more or less guilty of this error than many other evolutionary youthful genera. But as a race we are just approaching spiritual adolescence and should start to look beyond ourselves and our own limitations for the answers.

Our friends within the parallel universe appear in many forms, some of which are easily recognizable as so-termed mythological beasts from folklore and fable. According to the ancient Greek teachings, it was to two of these fabulous strains in particular that the task fell to fill the tutorial role to both gods and men. These were the satyrs and centaurs. Both represent a merging point between human and animal consciousness, with the best and wisest traits of both predominating. Sometimes the ancients gave certain of them names which have been handed down to us over the centuries; Silenus and Chiron, for example. But there are many other willing tutors among them, and from first hand experience we may assure the aspiring Hero that they are never slow to come forward, make their purpose known and identify themselves. Just as the tutelary divinity watches over his or her charge, so the role of the tutor, in addition to being informative, is to teach the aspiring Hero how to evaluate each experience in an initiatory light. Of course there will come a point at which the aspiring Hero bids his tutor farewell for, as Nietzche so wisely commented 'One repays a teacher badly if one remains always a pupil.' But by that time the goal will be well and truly in sight.

If you find this whole tale strains your credulity, then the Heroic Path is not for you. There were none more logical than the Greek masters, and if the minds of Plato and Pythagoras could grasp these principles and logicize them, then any deficiency we may suffer from in this direction should not be blamed on logic, but rather on limited programming and mental conditioning. The human brain is, as we have already stressed, constructed to accommodate an easy comprehension of dimensions of this kind without fear or apprehension and, as long as these realms are ventured into under strict mental control and not via the way of false stimulants, then the aspiring Hero has nothing to fear. But should the reverse be the case, then the phantoms encountered will not be a benign and wise old Chiron, or a stern but humorous Silenus, or a smiling, healing Pan! Forewarned is forearmed, so enter these realms at your own peril!

No, you do not have to seek your tutor. That is not part of the initiation. In keeping with the old adage, 'When the pupil is ready the master appears', he or she will come to *you*. But you must find your god or goddess who will, in turn, make you the gift of a magical instrument or weapon. This could be any of those we shall illustrate in a future chapter, or something designed by the deity exclusively for you, the aspiring Hero. Thus well armed, protected and watched over, you may take your first tottering steps. The experience may seem bewildering initially, but then comes the exhilaration as the higher frequencies start to purify your mind and the clear light drops the scales from your eyes. Of course you will stumble; no tutor or guiding deity would have it any other way, for how else would you learn? But after each bruising the right balm will be handed to you, plus the staff or weapon necessary for negotiating the next encounter that lurks just around the bend . . .

14. THE OCCULT NATURES AND FUNCTIONS OF THE TWELVE OLYMPIANS

Here we are dealing strictly with the twelve Olympians. Although other minor deities were later admitted to the *sanctum sanctorum*, Dionysus and Hercules, for example, these are viewed more in the light of heroic examples which serve to show the Initiate just how it can be done. So let us commence with the father of the gods himself:

ZEUS

Descriptive Archetype: Patriarchal father.

Qualities: Justice. Leadership. Popularity.

Areas of Activity: The Establishment. The Law.

Colour: Imperial purple.

Symbols: Oak tree. Thunderbolt. Eagle.

Zeus is invoked for assistance in any of the above mentioned areas of life. Injustice may be presented to him and grievances of any kind laid at his feet. He dispenses his judgments via his messengers. These may be minor deities such as Iris, the Winds, or other Olympians: Apollo or Hermes, for example. If your role in life is an authoritarian or legal one, think in terms of Zeus as your patron.

HERA

Descriptive Archetype: Queenly, aristocratic lady. Faithful wife.

Qualities: Fidelity. Endurance. Conjugal love.

Areas of Activity: The organization of the home and all situations where a lady can play a helpful but equal part with her husband or committed partner.

Colour: Emerald green.

Symbols: Sceptre surmounted by a cuckoo. Pomegranate. Peacock.

Hera is the divinity whose aid one should seek when faced with situations where infidelity would appear to be rife and insecurity is the basis of the problem. Her story tells us that although one cannot change the basic nature of man one can gently channel it into constructive avenues, there being no advantage to be gained in the long run by spite or vengeance.

ATHENE

Descriptive Archetype: All-powerful but wise female warrior.

Qualities: Strength. Wisdom. Healing. Creative skills.

Areas of Activity: Music (she invented the flute). Military matters, but only in the cause of true justice. Weaving and embroidery. Protection, both psychic and physical.

Colour: Red-gold.

Symbols: The magical spear. Golden helmet. Aegis. Shield or protective breastplate. Flute. Owl.

The energies of this dual aspected goddess are available upon request both to the aspiring Hero and ordinary person alike. Patron of career ladies in particular, Athene can bestow crafts and skills for the domestic scene, as well as magical weapons for the spiritual warrior. Her shield acts in the same way as Hathor's mirror; it reflects back negative energies on the sender. Perseus learned from Athene never to look an enemy directly in the eye — and that lesson goes for us all. If malice is your foe, but your heart is true, Athene will always oblige with the loan of her famous shield. Her lesson is that strength alone never achieved any real peace and, in the final analysis, battle for its own sake is the game of fools and young souls.

APOLLO

Descriptive Archetype: Beautiful, golden-haired solar man. Patron of prophecy, art and music.

Qualities: Harmony. Charisma. Beauty. Musical talent. Healing.

Areas of Activity: Natural healing. The arts. Divination.

Colour: Yellow-gold.

Symbols: Lyre. Bow and arrow. Dolphin. All divinatory aids.

Apollo has power over the serpent of darkness, radiance always counteracting its opposite. His celestial arrows, being infallible, always find their target. Likewise, his energies can help the aspiring Hero to home onto his target. But Apollo's special message is that the best way to achieve spiritual aims is through the avenues of music and harmony. His devotion to his sister, Artemis, and their joint caring for their mother, Leto, also carries a strong significance which should be pondered upon and fully understood.

ARTEMIS

Descriptive Archetype: Inviolate virgin. Huntress of souls. Animal lover.

Qualities: Purity. Reliability.

Areas of Activity: Protection, particularly psychic. The animal and elemental kingdoms.

Colour: Amethyst.

Symbols: Bow and arrow (which she shares with her brother, Apollo). Torch. Animals in general, but especially the cat, dog, bear and hind.

This goddess is particularly concerned with the safety and welfare of women who are receiving unwelcome male attention. Like her brother she has strong family connections, especially with her mother. As a protector against psychic attack she is without equal and her skill with the bow and arrow is commensurate with that of her brother. She is also patron of singers. Invoke her aid when you are faced with the necessity to negotiate those places in the universe where the spirits of men are not predominant. This would apply to the animal and elemental kingdoms on this planet, or to the realms of the fabulous beasts and those unfamiliar evolutionary strains the aspiring Hero will inevitably encounter during his or her cosmic explorations. Her friends are the wood nymphs and she knows the deep, secret places of nature wherein one can rest and gather strength before facing the next affray. The Earth's chakras come under her special care. If you feel a close affinity with the animal or elemental kingdoms, Artemis is the tutelary deity for you.

HERMES

Descriptive Archetype: Slim, athletic man. Celestial messenger and traveller.

Qualities: Speed. Ingenuity. Intelligence. Healing.

Areas of Activity: Commerce. Travel. Learning and knowledge. Medicine. Diplomacy.

Colour: Silver.

Symbols: Caduceus. Winged hat. Winged sandals.

Hermes is god of orthodox or rational medicine, also all things practical and commercial. He guides the traveller spiritually, intellectually and practically and his energies are closely linked with the gift of speech, wit and articulation. When at a loss for words, lost during a journey, or seeking essential knowledge, you may request his assistance. His caduceus will also help to rebalance a situation that has become one-sided, be it in relation to health, business or any form of negotiation. Should your chosen lot in this life involve travel, business, journalism, diplomacy or medicine, give Hermes a little thought . . . he might be just right for you.

ARES

Descriptive Archetype: Tough, macho, insensitive warrior.

Qualities: Raw energy. Brute strength. Untamed passion.

Areas of Activity: Battle of any kind, or any situation where sheer stamina is needed.

Colour: Scarlet.

Symbols: All weapons of war.

Ares should only be invoked when the aspiring Hero has mastered the use of pure energy, otherwise the Martian force will proceed no further than his lower chakra (*Muladhara*), where it will manifest as violence for its own sake, or as unbridled sex. However, when the Initiate feels ready to negotiate this particular force-field in the safe knowledge that it will not knock him backwards, the strength to be gained may manifest in industry, stamina and determination. There are occasions when Ares can be of great help in a world where violence is rife and the only language understood by some is the one which they themselves speak. The 'presence' of Ares can prove very deterring to a would-be assailant of low intelligence who worships brute force for its own sake. Ares can also help you to keep going when you feel the last drop of strength is about to leave you. He could prove a very helpful guide and mentor for the timid soul who is sometimes too gentle to cope with the brutal adversities of life!

HEPHAESTUS

Descriptive Archetype: Short, swarthy, broad-shouldered smith.

Qualities: Manual dexterity. Conscientiousness. Hard work. Inventiveness.

Areas of Activity: All creative crafts, engineering, building, construction.

Colour: Bronze.

Symbols: Conical bonnet. Hammer and tongs. The net.

Hephaestus, like the Egyptian Ptah, is very much the ordinary man's deity. His energies relate to the sort of skills which bring comfort and joy to daily living. These range from heavy construction at one end of the scale to the creation of intricate jewellery or micro-electronics at the other. He is invoked for all practical matters which involve any form of manual dexterity or inventiveness. A good tutelary deity for the practical, technical man or woman.

APHRODITE

Descriptive Archetype: Beautiful, fair-haired, seductive love goddess.

Qualities: Sensuality. Generosity. Passion. Pure love.

Areas of Activity: All forms of partnership or relationship.

Colour: Turquoise blue.

Symbols: The girdle or zona.

In spite of what might appear in the myths as a frivolous personality, at the higher frequencies Aphrodite is anything but this. Of course, as with all magical practices, the student is only able to contact that level of the principle that he or she is capable of handling at any one period in his or her initiation. Aphrodite's powers can obviously be invoked for seductive purposes to aid relationships, or simply for 'kicks' but, as with the employment of all energies from other dimensions, the avenues into which they are channelled will always set up a positive reaction which will inevitably be mirrored back on the user. So call upon Aphrodite for the cause of true, cosmic love and the power of her girdle will lay the universe at your feet. But fall short of that ideal and you can expect to receive back exactly what you give out!

POSEIDON

Descriptive Archetype: A mature, bearded man, enthroned on or beneath the waves.

Qualities: Intuition. Movement. Fluidity.

Areas of Activity: The human emotions. All things associated with the seas: ships and those who sail in them.

Colour: Coral.

Symbols: Conch shell. White horse. Trident. Fish.

Poseidon represents the great collective unconscious from which we may all draw information, if we know how. Learning to probe these depths was likened by the ancients to the ability to dwell beneath the seas without drowning. In other words, understanding the true meaning of 'feeling' without sinking into the morass of emotionalism that can swamp so many of us here on this planet. *Homo sapiens* is more strongly associated with the Element of Water than the other three Elements. Water, therefore, and all that it stands for, exerts a tremendous influence over man, as he is basically an emotional animal. If you, the aspiring Hero, are naturally intellectual (airy), forceful and creative (fiery), or intensely practical (earthy), seek the tutelary favours of Poseidon if you wish to secure your fourfold nature, that being a necessary prerequisite for your ascent to Olympus.

HESTIA

Descriptive Archetype: A gentle, reserved, maiden lady or nun.

Qualities: Discipline. Dedication to duty. Humility. Modesty. Prudence. Acceptance. Continuity.

Areas of Activity: The home and hearth, therefore the family. But also the cloister and those 'orders' in life wherein people have chosen to serve others while also retaining the respect and esteem of those they serve.

Colour: White.

Symbols: The flaming circle. The veil. The domestic hearth or fireplace.

This is the tutelary goddess for the dedicated servant of humanity who is far past the ego-tripping stage. Mother Teresa of Calcutta could be described as a 'Hestia' person. If you, the aspiring Hero or Heroine, have chosen Hestia to accompany you on your Olympic journey, your monsters may not be dragons, gorgons or serpents, but the draconian legislation of uncaring authorities, the ugliness of poverty and disease, and the cunning of those who would like to see you out of the way.

DEMETER

Descriptive Archetype: A beautiful, but grave, mature woman in the maternal mode.

Qualities: Maternal love. Caring. Fertility. Multiplication. Magical philosophy.

Areas of Activity: Anywhere in life where fertility and fecundity are of prime importance.

Colour: Cornflower blue.

Symbols: Ears of corn. Torch.

The Demeter 'ray' is one of those occultly interesting wave lengths that can manifest on a purely practical level as fertility, expansion, plenty, etc., while its upper frequencies encompass the force-fields of higher magic and magical philosophy. In other words, as with all archetypal principles its energies naturally relate to the level at which it is being employed. For the average Athenian of old, Demeter represented the harvest and all that it stood for; but to the sage she was like the Egyptian Isis, mistress of magic, the philosophy behind which is concerned with the manifestation of the multiplication principle at all levels. As the story of Demeter so beautifully illustrates, however, expansion can oft-times be painful in that it demands sacrifice.

* * *

The number '12' is highly significant in Greek magic. In fact, a deeper insight into the actual nature of the twelve Olympians can prove very revealing. There are six males and six females and it may be observed that three of each group emphasize the *anima* or female aspect of the nature, and three the *animus* or masculine side, in both males and females. The outward affirmation of these traits as expressed introvertedly or extrovertedly is endorsed in their activities:

Goddesses		Gods	
Aphrodite	... *anima* (Extrovert)	Zeus	... *animus* (Extrovert)
Hera	... *anima* (Introvert)	Ares	... *animus* (Extrovert)
Demeter	... *anima* (Introvert)	Hephaestus	... *animus* (Introvert)
Athene	... *animus* (Extrovert)	Apollo	... *anima* (Extrovert)
Artemis	... *animus* (Introvert)	Hermes	... *anima* (Extrovert)
Hestia	... *animus* (Introvert)	Poseidon	... *anima* (Introvert)

In other words, we are being given some fine examples of how the human spirit may manifest to best advantage in either a male or female body, employing either the *anima* or *animus* emphatically to express its true nature. The *animus*-motivated goddesses are inevitably virgins, inferring the predominance of reason over the emotions, while the other three are all emotionally-orientated mothers. Among the gods, the artistic Apollo, detached Hermes and deeply emotional Poseidon display the *anima*, while the overtly macho Zeus and Ares join with Hephaestus, the craftsman, to represent the emphasized *animus*. Interesting, is it not?

15. WORKING WITH THE MINOR DEITIES, FABULOUS BEASTS AND NATURE DIVINITIES

All the powers of the minor deities, mythical beasts, elements and spirits of nature are available for the aspiring Hero's use as the gods may deem fit. Although they may not merit the same emphasis as the 'twelve', their energies serve in positive ways, as far as the Path of Initiation is concerned.

In Chapter 4 a few identities are supplied not all of which, however, are of occult interest or relevance, so let us now sort the magical wheat from the mythological chaff.

Hades

The aspiring Hero will sooner or later find himself doomed to visit the regions of Hades. This carries a dual significance: one aspect relating to his ability to negotiate the lower astral in safety and security, and the other appertaining to his eventual mastery over death and the necessity to eliminate all fear of that state from his understanding. Once he has attained to the former he will win the right to borrow Hades' Helmet of Invisibility which will confer upon him the power of astral projection so that he may travel mentally where he wishes without fear of detection. But the latter he will not overcome until he is well up the Olympian mountain.

There are two further Hadean obstacles to be dealt with: firstly Cerberus, whose good offices he will *never* court with brute force but only, as the tale of Orpheus tells us, by way of beauty and gentleness; and, secondly, the trap that lies in the seductive glances of wealth and riches. Extricate himself from these and Hades' subterranean regions will be open for him to come and go at will, by which time, however, he will have no further need to pay the old chap any further calls.

Dionysus

Dionysus being 'twice-born', or 'the child of the double door', emphasizes the transformatory nature of his energies. The control of this ray, therefore, calls for the elimination of any offending *cacoethes* which must be faced up to and dealt with before the aspiring Hero can progress beyond the foothills of Olympus, its significance, as far as the human condition is concerned, having already been discussed. Once mastery of this aspect of the 'self' has been attained the aspiring Hero may then number the Thyrsus among his magical attributes, but until such times the illusions presented by false stimulants and bodily malfunctions aggravated by incorrect diet will continue to plague him.

Pan

So important is this divinity that he has been allotted a chapter to himself (see Chapter 16).

Iris

If it has not already become obvious from our earlier summary of this goddess and her attributes, Iris represents the telepathic contact between Olympus and the other worlds, including that of mankind. Her message, as far as the aspiring Hero is concerned, is that as long as a close mental link with the gods is maintained, all initiatory storms end in a silver lining. The rainbow, therefore, constitutes a strong and encouraging link between the finite and the infinite and speaks for the occult part to be played by Iris.

Satyrs and Centaurs

The tutorial role assigned to these personalities has already been established. The fact that they are portrayed as half-man and half-beast is highly significant. The upper or human part denotes their ability to see into the mind of man and read his innermost thoughts, for how otherwise could they hope to teach him the way of the gods? The lower half represents the instinctive or animal nature over which their species has already gained domination through the use of logic and reason. They are, therefore, perfectly able to feel and think as *both* man and beast, having complete understanding of man's lower and higher natures. The manner in which these beings are visualized and their genus interpreted will reflect the nature and stage of development of the viewer. Therefore, he whose mind produces the blurred picture of an inebriated *roué* is seeing only himself reflected in his own inner vision. But, to the sagacious aspiring Hero the satyrs and centaurs are anything but that!

Another essential task they fulfil, along with other fabulous beasts such as Pegasus, is to provide the aspirant with a clearer perspective regarding his role in the universal scheme of things, the inference being (as with Pegasus and Bellerophon) that man alone does not own the path to Olympus, many a stranger-looking creature (by man's standards) having made it well ahead of him.

The Muses

Each Muse has been assigned a specific area of human activity, as may be noted in Chapter 17. The aspiring Hero who specializes in any of these areas may seek the aid of the associated Muse and employ her symbology. But, remember, the Muses are the servants of Apollo, so if he is your tutelary deity you will have easy access to them. This, of course, applies to any of the minor divinities who form part of the retinue of an Olympian. The Graces, for example, serve Aphrodite and will therefore favour those who have chosen to tread the Olympian path under her tutelage.

The Fates

An understanding of the Laws of Karma is essential to the aspiring Hero. These he may learn, to some degree, from the Moerae under the direction of his tutor. We say 'to some degree' because a full comprehension of Karmic Law is not really possible for the spirit incarnate in the body of *Homo sapiens*. Only when that soul is freed from the wheel of Karma and exposed to the truths of the infinite universe does the full picture become obvious. The mind of man is continually clouded by emotion (Water), conditioned reasoning (Air), irrational idealism (Fire) and over-possessiveness (Earth), so it is little wonder that the broader karmic picture may appear at times unjust and bewildering to him.

Which leads us to the next and most important contact for the aspiring Hero to effect, and that is with the four Elements of Air, Fire, Earth and Water. Until man has gained his fourfold nature he cannot hope to break the karmic chain that binds him to birth and rebirth in the sphere of gross matter and, like Sisyphus, he will find himself wearily pushing his earthly boulder up the mountain side only to have it roll down again as soon as he reaches the summit.

The four Elements are the habitat of a life form broadly dubbed 'devic'. The spirits of these Elements have been assigned names that are recognized by occultists: the inhabitants of the fiery experience are called Salamanders; the airy beings, Sylphs; those of water, Ondines; while the denizens of the deep places of Earth are designated Gnomes (see *Practical Techniques of Psychic Self-Defence*). The Greeks of old were well aware of these facts and accorded the elemental forces the respect they deserve. After all, it is with their permission that we exist, the very substance of our bodies being formed from their regions.

Man also carries within him the potential for mastering the principles they represent, each Element having specific qualities ascribed to it in human terms. The Salamanders are associated with creativity, ardour, raw energy, valour and loyalty; the Sylphs with intellectuality, speed, communication, detachment and inventiveness; the Ondines with emotions, feelings, receptivity, understanding and sympathy; and the Gnomes with thrift, acquisition, wealth in all forms, conservation and practicality.

The four 'humours' or psychological types, as outlined by Hippocrates, are also assigned to the Elements: Fire — the Sanguine; Air — the Bilious; Water — the Phlegmatic; and Earth — the Melancholic. The aspiring Hero would do well to examine his or her own psychology to see in which of these avenues of expression he is either well-endowed or is lacking. That which comes easily to him represents what he has already mastered and the elemental force associated with its principle will therefore make its offices more readily available for his magical usage. But that which he lacks must be learned or acquired somewhere along the upward path before he will win the admiration, respect and help of those who inhabit its associated energy field.

Although the elemental forces function mainly in group form, spirits from among them may individuate to aid the Initiate and, in so doing, assist their own evolutionary progress which, as with *Homo sapiens*, involves breaking at some point from their 'collective'. In achieving that break they also learn to experience through the minds and feelings of other life forms until they, too, gain their fourfold nature and are then free to ascend to the higher kingdoms of devas or angels. Individualized elemental spirits rule powerful pockets of the elemental group force. The Greeks gave them names, as with the four winds. The aspiring Hero is advised to listen carefully to the voice of the wind, as the messages of the gods are frequently carried on its wings.

The nymphs, of course, correspond to the Ondines although, as has already been commented upon, the term 'nymph' in Greek mythology is used to cover a multitude of beings.

Dryads, or tree spirits, come under the rulership of what are broadly termed the Pan kingdoms, which include the spirits or life forces behind all growing things. Although plants, flowers or crops of this Earth may be tended by Gnomes, Sylphs or whatever, they are an evolutionary stream unto themselves. The aspiring Hero must have a full understanding of and sympathy with the kingdoms of nature, and this means respecting everything from the tiniest bud to the tallest tree! As the awareness increases, love will grow and nature, being always reflective, will return that love with interest according to the quality of its own bounty. The man who is in harmony with nature and the Elements is strong indeed: a veritable Hercules . . . !

16. THE NATURE AND POWER OF PAN

The recent spate of general interest in all matters ecological has brought home to many an occult student the need to know and understand more about the nature kingdoms. Years of urban living tend to destroy man's sensitivity towards species other than his own, a neglect which has produced more mental illness than could possibly be imagined; so people have slowly started to turn their attention to the voice of nature prompted, perhaps, by the need for its healing energies, or simply as an escape from the stress-filled life of the city rat race. Once rid of the ravages of that thousand-headed giant named 'noise' the human spirit is free to rediscover the other intelligences with whom it shares this planet, the advantages gained by so doing being legion.

We have already considered the origins of Pan and the false information rendered from the past regarding his 'death'. But, upon reflection, was that information so very wrong? Surely man had killed him off, albeit temporarily, by his very denial of the god's existence. In other words, by rejecting the importance of and the role played by the Pan kingdoms and those intelligences that inhabit them, man has succeeded in isolating himself from an essential aspect of both his own nature and the very planet which provides him with the stuff of existence. To believe in something is to contribute towards its life energies; thoughts are 'things' and the power of thought is infinite. As we grow in our knowledge and understanding of the gods they expand through us. Taking into account that in the eternal 'now' all is happening simultaneously, however, from their position in time they are all-knowing; it is only we ourselves, as isolated fragments encapsulated in the time zone called the present, who cannot see or comprehend the whole.

Pan is said to be the deva who rules over all the spirits of nature on this planet. People working in small, selective groups have managed to make contact with the Pan force as personalized in the form of the old 'goat-man'. Of course, this does not imply that Pan actually looks like that; the 'goat-man' guise is simply a 'suit of clothes' in which man has seen fit to garb him. But it would appear that he has no objection, as long as he is acknowledged in one form or another. There are several heavily loaded magical questions regarding the Pan archetype that call for explanation:

1. His vocal powers: the silvery Pan voice is said to contain powerful properties which could shatter the ears of all but the adept. True or false?

Half and half, the legend obviously containing a folk memory of a time in the long past when sonics employed in growth stimulation might well have irritated the ears of those who had not been slowly accustomed to their frequencies. But Pan, as the individuated nature force, can sit beside a small child and chat happily with no ill effects to the little one whatsoever.

2. If Pan should appear to you he will always sit at your side, because it is unwise to look him straight in the eyes. True or false?

Again, half and half. The Pan ray is what is termed a 'mirror' ray; in other words, it reflects back anything it encounters. If Pan should choose to seat himself beside you in some wooded glade or gentle lea and not look you directly in the eye, the inference would be that he deems you unready for the experience of seeing yourself for what you truly are. If, on the other hand, he should sit before you and confront you face to face, than you are well and truly on the path of Olympian ascent.

3. Pan may be summoned by ritual, but only by an adept of superior rank, such as a magus or ipsissimus. True or false?

False! Aleister Crowley's notorious Paris 'working' comes to mind, alleged reports of which tend to strain the credulity to say the least. The aforementioned ranks are only the invention of one group of men anyway and do not necessarily bear any real relationship to true human spirituality. While the heroic aspirant is reminded to respect the ways and beliefs of other pursuants of the magical path, he is in no way obliged to accept them as valid terms of reference for himself. Preference must always be given to the instructions of the tutor and inner visions bestowed by the Olympian tutelary divinity. This is not to say that Pan may not be summoned by ritual, but that will depend on who is carrying out the ceremony. A small, innocent child may call Pan and he will come without hesitation. The ability to learn certain rituals by heart does not guarantee the student occultist the right of access to the ways of the gods, any more than a doctorate degree in medicine makes for a good physician. The ability to memorize facts and the gift of wisdom are *not* synonymous!

4. The famous Pan call. Is there anything in it and, if so, what?

Yes, there is and here it is. The Pan call consists of a series of four notes which relate to the four Elements. Although it was originally played on the flute, any wind instrument may be used, or it can be sung with the human voice. It was taught to Arcadian shepherds in olden times and is no doubt as potent today as it was then. The sequence in which the notes are rendered is highly important and related to what is musically termed the Lydian mode. It can be transposed into any key which accommodates its sounds, but for convenience and to facilitate reference at this point we recommend it in the key of F minor, with the notes of F, G, C and E flat. Anyone wishing to transpose it should note that the sequence runs one, two, five, with the flattened seventh making up the fourth or upper note.

Does it work? Yes, it does; but a hasty warning! *Pan should never be summoned unless his aid is genuinely required.* His energies, which have been described as 'radioactive', are highly stimulating and if unused when invoked can cause havoc, both to the ill-advised practitioner and anyone else likely to frequent the spot for some time afterwards. The correct way to employ the Pan ray is either for healing (his powers are particularly effective in cases of fever where the sickness is caused by a bacteria or virus) or where a genuine growth stimulus is needed. There are those people who dare to call themselves occultists who would think nothing of invoking Pan just to see what happens. It is little wonder that any manifestations obtained under such indifferent circumstances have earned the god an ill reputation. By the Laws of Magic, when an energy is invoked or evoked it *must* be used or sent somewhere, otherwise it will rebound on whoever issued the summons.

But on the bright and happy side Pan is anything but sinister. Wishing to erase all knowledge of him forever, the early Christians painted their devil in the image and likeness of the goat-man god, but little good did it do them. A lie will out sooner or later and the oncoming tide of religious rationalism is doing a fine job of laying the ghost of 'old Nick' to rest once and for all.

As a nature deity Pan is more than willing to kneel beside the man or woman who lovingly tends his or her plants, or to watch over the farmer as he sows his seeds. One does not need to be an adept, ritual magician or the like in order to court his good offices, but just to be oneself and openly and honestly give him love and acknowledgment. He will do the rest. The great god Pan lives . . . he is immortal!

17. THE MAJOR SYMBOLS EMPLOYED IN HEROIC MAGIC

Every magical system or tradition has its own special symbology, which is either based upon the interpretation of the individuated energies most favoured by its practitioners, or the god/angelic forms originally designated as being responsible for its inception and growth. Certain symbols are, however, common to all occult schools, being more universal in flavour and not the limited by-product of any one ethnic group or location. Greek magic, too, has its special emblems, plus a few of the more cosmic variety, as we shall see, the following being the most useful and effective for the aspiring Hero and layman alike.

Bow and Arrow

Representing the *anima* and *animus*, or outgoing and receptive aspects of the personality, the Bow and Arrow are symbolic of aiming for a target, seeking out new fields of endeavour, or hunting for the 'self'. As attributes of Apollo they are said to stand for the Sun's energy, its rays and its fertilizing and purifying powers. The tension necessary for the shooting of an arrow suggests the testing grounds of experience; when we are stretched to our very limits we achieve the furthest distance. The early Greek culture was not the only one to employ the arrow to suggest the Sun's rays; it can also be found in this context in pre-Columbian America. Phallic inferences have obviously crept into its meaning at the

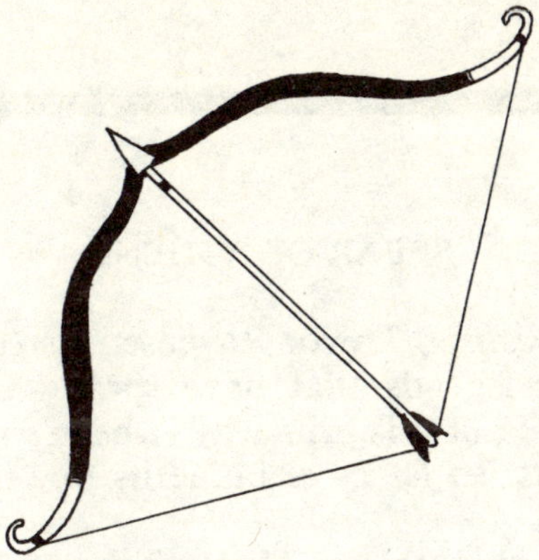

BOW AND ARROW

lower levels, as with Shiva's bow, but this is the case with most symbols which can be interpreted at several levels.

Magically, the Bow and Arrow should be used in the 'seeking' context rather than as a defensive or aggressive weapon. When unsure of a situation, or needing an answer, attach your request to an arrow and send it to Apollo or Artemis. It will shortly return to you in some very natural way with an appropriate reply.

Much of what is broadly termed 'evil' is misplaced or misappropriated energy; the Bow and Arrow can provide an excellent magical instrument for disposing of or dispersing same. Mentally encapsulate the manifestation in a sealed bag or small container, shrinking it to an appropriate size by mind visualization. Then attach it to your arrow and let fly, aiming at where you feel it should rightfully belong. If unsure, always ask Apollo or Artemis to guide your shaft.

Spear of Athene

As distinct from the sword, the spear has deeper connotations. It was a spear, we are told, that pierced the side of Christ at the Crucifixion, causing blood and water to flow therefrom. Water is always an emotional indicator, so here we are given an example of the spear's employment in the emotional release that comes with death and the separation from the encumbrance of the physical vehicle. In his book,

SPEAR OF ATHENE

The Spear of Destiny, Trevor Ravenscroft recounts many of the myths and legends that have sprung up around that particular spear. But it is primarily Athene's magical weapon that concerns us, so let us examine its powers in the Greek magical context.

Athene was able to fell Ares with one blow. Athene represents wisdom; Ares, brute strength; and yet both were warriors. War is simply an exchange of destructive energies, during which both sides stand to lose. Sometimes the vanquished gains more than the victor, so there must be a point in this consideration at which logic takes over. Athene did not like fighting for its own sake, she simply engaged in it to help someone out or to assist a just cause. Her real preference was for her more domestic activities of weaving and embroidery. Wisdom, the myth is telling us, sometimes needs to meet force at its own level in order to pursue the path to more peaceful ways. By its very nature it will eventually triumph for, as evolution progresses, the lower energy frequencies, and everything that goes with them, must be left behind.

Another interesting point is that Athene, the supreme warrior, was a woman, inferring it will be women who will eventually triumph over male-dominated aggression, after which they will be able to return to their domestic pursuits in the safe knowledge that war is no more. Jung believed the Aquarian Age to be the age of the ascendancy of woman during which intuition, caring and the finer qualities of the *anima* would become manifest at the expense (hopefully) of macho brutality. Athene's Spear represents, therefore, the power that releases those emotional waters of feeling and intuition that can overcome brute force. Ladies, therein lies your power; for those men who would also like to see the dawning of a gentler age, the energies of the Spear are yours to use if you can forget your over-emphasized *animus* and call your *anima* to the fore.

The aspiring Hero should employ this magical weapon as a defence against overt aggression, with the emphasis on the word 'defence'. Raise your magical Spear when you are under attack from negative forces and Athene will receive your message and hasten to your aid. Sleep with it always (mentally) by your side and reach for it in times of crisis.

Cornucopia

Fashioned from the horn of the goat Amaltheia, whom Zeus placed in the heavens as the constellation of Capricorn in gratitude for services rendered, the Cornucopia, or horn of plenty, contained an inexhaustible supply of whatever food or drink was required. It is a reminder that when we give or render a service to the gods they repay us in more ways than we could possibly conceive. Giving and receiving is an exchange of energies, a barter which is essential for the continuance of the universe in accordance with the Law of Abundance.

In magical usage it represents the inexhaustible or infinite flow of cosmic energy that is always there for the taking, as long as we are familiar with the necessary *modus operandi* for drawing it down and condensing it into a frequency or mode that is applicable to our particular need. Amaltheia can help here (most Capricornians know how to handle money and material goods!) in the same way that she aided the infant

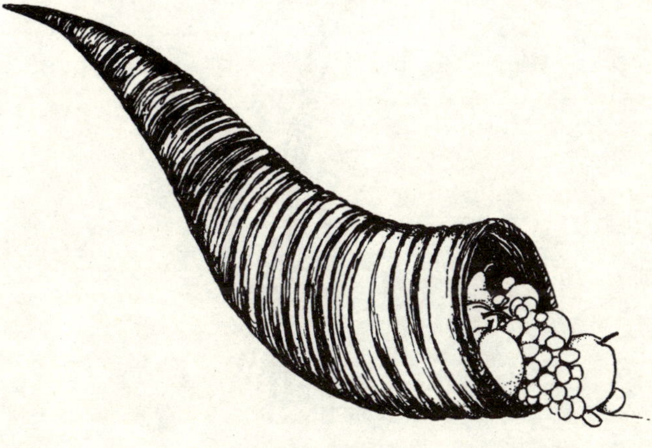

CORNUCOPIA

Zeus. Or you can always ask Zeus to intercede with her on your behalf. But, in truth, the aspiring Hero need never go without the essentials of life if he or she observes the Cornucopia code.

Ears of Corn

These may be woven into a corn dolly or presented in any recognizable 'harvest' form. Sacred to Demeter, they symbolize fertility and fecundity, but are by no means exclusive to the Greek magical system. However, as Demeter's main attribute, they constitute an essential emblem

EARS OF CORN

for use in her rites, and the aspirant to her Mysteries would do well to incorporate them into his or her personal symbology. Demeter's energies, although also related to nature, are of a quite different texture to those of Pan, the Pan 'ray' being stimulative rather than reproductive. So while Demeter showers the Earth with verdant growth, bright flowers and the fruits of the harvest, it is the denizens of Pan's kingdoms that assist her work by caring for it and stimulating its development.

The Ears of Corn can be employed separately or incorporated into the Cornucopia. Either way will be acceptable to the goddess and will encourage her beneficence. But it should be borne in mind that fecundity in itself does not constitute the complete attainment. All growing things need to be carefully tended and wisely harvested so that their fruits may become available to all who would need them. So while Demeter will be more than happy to oblige anyone who seeks her good offices, the end results must always be accounted for in terms of personal growth experience, fertility of mind and bounty rendered to others.

Aegis

Another attribute that originated with Amaltheia, the Aegis was fashioned from her hide (or some say from the skin of the giant Pallas) and constituted a breastplate which no arrow

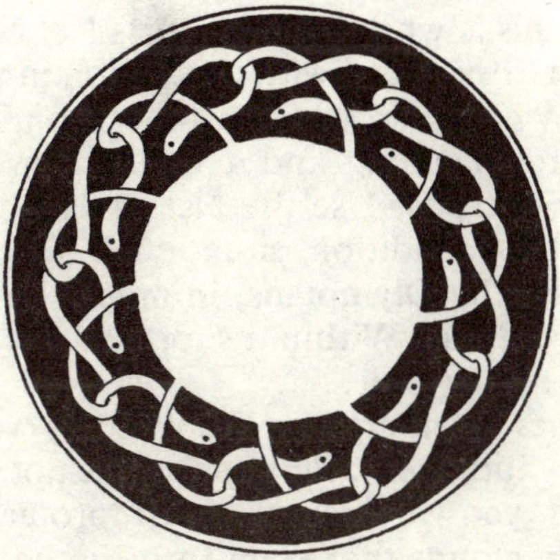

AEGIS

could pierce. Zeus used it for the first time during his fight with the Titans, after which he presented it to his daughter, Athene, who usually wore it slung over her shoulder. It is shown as a sort of cuirass, fringed and bordered with snakes, and bearing in the centre the head of the gorgon, Medusa.

This picture which the myths present to us suggests a horrifying sort of garment, guaranteed to put the fear of the gods into anyone! But what are they really trying to tell us? Surely this is a variation of Athene's fabled Shield, which reflects the image of the attacker back onto himself. Shield and Aegis are, in fact, one symbol and, as has been previously mentioned, the aspiring Hero should always arm him or herself with a protective cloak of some sort, be it the shining Shield that the goddess loaned to Perseus, or the terrifying Aegis that is guaranteed to discourage would-be assailants in the first place. A gorgon's head, being hardly a comfortable symbol upon which to meditate, we have designed our own Aegis in the form of a shield which incorporates the serpent theme with the reflective rays of the sun of enlightenment. So, aspiring Hero, you can take your pick.

Net of Hephaestus

We have already seen how Hephaestus used his carefully forged Net to entrap his wayward spouse and her Martian lover. But for the pursuant of the Greek magical path the Net has many other uses. Basically it is a holding symbol. There is an old saying in the north of England: 'When in doubt, do nought'. And this is when Hephaestus's Net comes in handy. The occultist is often faced with a situation in which he or she is unsure as to what to do. No assistance from the gods would appear to be forthcoming and a wrong move at that point could prove disastrous. Use the Net of Hephaestus. Simply wrap it around the condition, situation or problem, and leave it in full view of the Olympians, in much the same way that the old smith god did. Within a short space of time you will receive the correct answer.

Circumstances often arise in life where it would be unwise to make a hasty judgment. Perhaps we are not in receipt of all the facts, and yet we feel we need protection from the brooding storm clouds that seem to be gathering around us. Fish out the jolly old Net and leave the situation safely encased therein. It will not be able to escape — in other

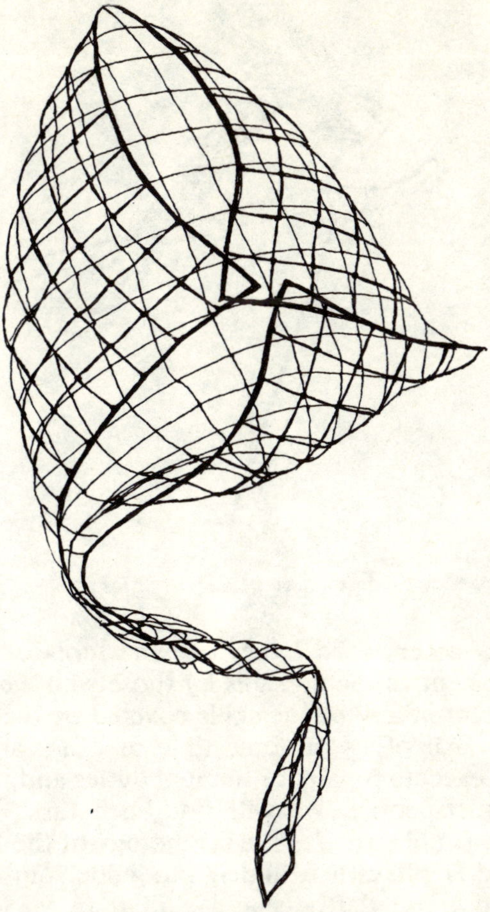

NET OF HEPHAESTUS

words, it will not develop overnight into an all-out thunderstorm any more than Zeus saw fit to hurl his bolts at Aphrodite and Ares. When the gods have considered the rights and wrongs they will tell you, so having used your Net you can relax and enjoy a good night's sleep.

Hammer and Tongs

The tools of Hephaestus, the craftsman, these symbols have the same uses at the earthly level as they do in the heavenly

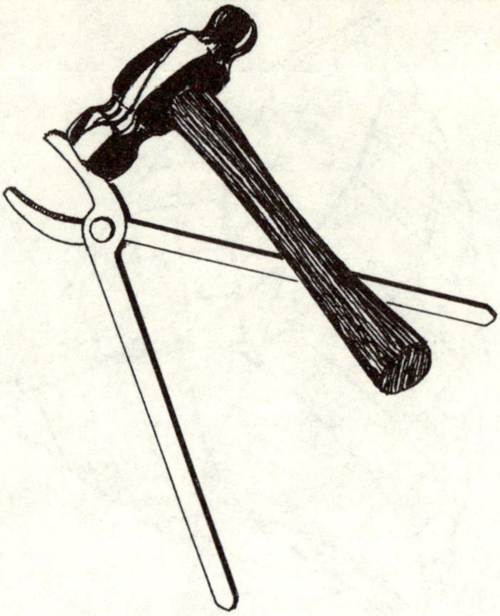

HAMMER AND TONGS

drama. In other words, they are the tools of a trade and should be kept as sacred sigils by those whose everyday lives involve them in any of the skills covered by the Hephaestian archetype. All of us at some time or other are faced with having to execute repairs or manual duties and, unless we are trained craftspeople, we will find such tasks onerous and beset with problems. Use the symbology of the Hammer and Tongs and Hephaestus will deign to guide your hands as you work with more deftness and skill than you might think yourself capable of. Tongs can pick up objects which might normally be too hot to handle, so use them magically if you are ever required to touch something of a psychic or occult nature that you feel to be of dubious origins or import. The Hammer is also the tool for putting things in their place, hammering in the nails or bending the metal of experience into shape in the heat of the refiner's fire. Hephaestus can help you to refine your spirit in the fire of his divine forge.

The Flaming Circle

Sacred to Hestia, the Circle represents eternity, the spiritual sun and the return to unity from multiplicity. The Gnostics

THE FLAMING CIRCLE

used the ouroboros or serpent eating its own tail to signify time and the continuity of life. In Greek magic Hestia's Circle emphasizes the continuing chain of existence, and also the sacred ring in which we may place ourselves to be protected by her divine fire. Hestia being a gentle and caring divinity, there is nothing aggressive about this symbol, which applies to the higher spiritual frequencies more than the more terrestrial levels. The explorer who is obliged to camp in inhospitable regions stokes his fires high before he retires for the night. In like manner the aspiring Hero may use Hestia's Circle for a safe night's sleep while on his quest of spiritual exploration; it will certainly serve to keep the wild beasts — both of the external and internal variety — well at bay.

Caduceus

In his *Dictionary of Symbols* Señor Cirlot, the eminent Spanish occultist, says of the Caduceus:

> A wand with two serpents twined round it, surmounted by two small wings or a winged helmet. The rational and historical explanation is the supposed intervention of Mercury in a fight between two serpents who thereupon curled themselves round his wand. For the Romans, the caduceus served as a symbol of

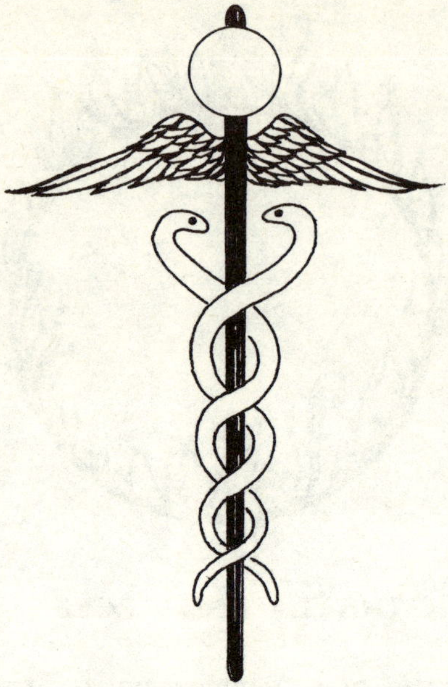

CADUCEUS

moral equilibrium and of good conduct. The wand represents power; the two snakes wisdom; the wings diligence; and the helmet is an emblem of lofty thoughts. Today the caduceus is the insignia of the Catholic bishop in the Ukraine. The caduceus also signifies the integration of the four elements, the wand corresponding to earth, the wings to air, the serpents to fire and water (by analogy with the undulating movement of waves and flames). This symbol is very ancient and is to be found for example in India engraved upon stone tablets called *nâgakals*, a kind of votive offering placed at the entrance to temples. Heinrich Zimmer traces the caduceus back to Mesopotamia, detecting it in the design of the sacrificial cup of King Gudea of Lagash (2600 BC). Zimmer even goes so far as to state that the symbol probably dates back beyond this period, for the Mesopotamians considered the intertwining serpents as a symbol of the god who cures all illness, a meaning which passed into Greek culture and is still preserved in emblems of our day. According to esoteric Buddhism the wand of the caduceus corresponds to the axis of the world and the serpents refer to the force called Kundalini which, in Tantrist teaching, sleeps coiled up at the base of the backbone — a symbol of the evolutive

> power of pure energy. Schneider maintains that the two S-shapes of the serpents correspond to illness and convalescence. In reality, what defines the essence of the caduceus is the nature and meaning not so much of its individual elements as of the composite whole. The precisely symmetrical and bilateral arrangement, as in the balance of Libra, or in the tri-unity of heraldry (a shield between two supporters), is always expressive of the same idea of acting equilibrium, of opposing forces balancing one another in such a way as to create a higher, static form. In the caduceus this balanced duality is twice stated: in the serpents and in the wings, thereby emphasizing that supreme state of strength and self-control (and consequently of health) which can be achieved both on the lower plane of the instincts (symbolized by the serpents) and on the higher level of the spirit (represented by the wings).

Care should be taken that the serpents cross at four points to represent the four Elements and not at three or even six, as in some portrayals. This is basically a healing symbol which invokes Hermes in his medical capacity. But as Hermes has other duties in the Greek system, it can also serve to tune one into the archetype at all levels. Should you be invoking our winged friend for commercial purposes, however, it is worth while bearing in mind that a true balancing of the situation might not be to your advantage. So examine your motives before employing the Caduceus for anything other than healing.

Trident

The attribute of Poseidon, the Trident has magical qualities of a 'claiming' nature. Legend has it that when the god wished to reclaim portions of land that had been annexed by Zeus or other gods he would strike his Trident into the ground, whereupon the inundating waters would once again ensure that it was returned to his domains. In palmistry, a trident in a certain position on the hand indicates that the person will never want, so there is also a strong good luck element about this symbol. When we wish to claim that which we feel to be rightly ours we may strike our Trident into the heart of the relevent situation, place, or condition of mind, but to employ Poseidon's emblem is to invoke his energies, so do not be surprised if he disagrees with your judgment! Poseidon's Trident can also quench the fires of destructive

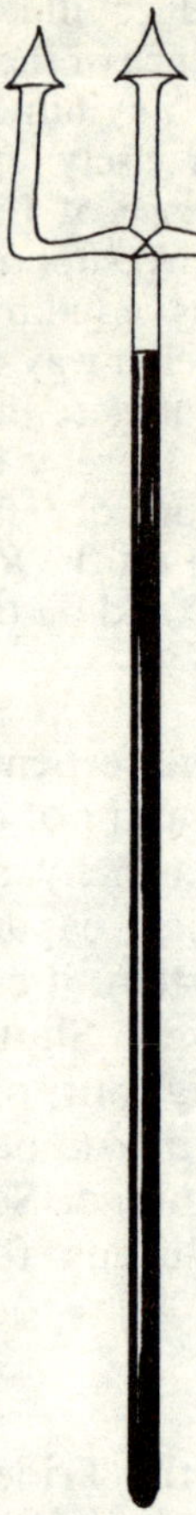

TRIDENT

passion and extinguish the sparks of anger that can sometimes make life difficult for us to bear. Of course it will work both ways, damping our own personal ardour and unwarranted passions and curbing our rising tempers. But the aspiring Hero must first control the monsters within himself before he can thrust his Trident into the encroaching enemy lines.

Zona or Girdle of Aphrodite
The cord, like the chain, is a general symbol for binding and connecting. In Egyptian hieroglyphics the knotted cord

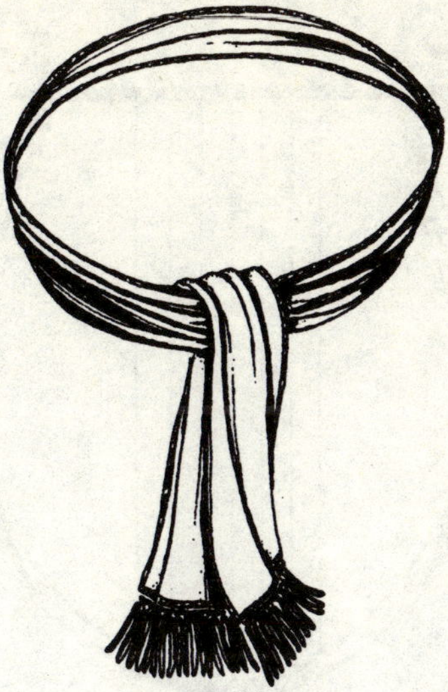

GIRDLE OF APHRODITE

signified a man's name, so it is interesting to find the cord or Girdle associated with the personification of the feminine principle, or goddess of love. It is, in fact, the most potent symbol in the whole of Greek magic, being more powerful than the thunderbolts of Zeus himself. The allegory is simple: love *is* the most potent and powerful force in the universe *if used in its purest context*. So often the word is bandied about to mean emotional or physical attraction or desire; use Aphrodite's Girdle at that level at your peril, would-be Hero, for as you sow so surely you will reap! But if your love is of the pure and universal kind nothing, *but nothing*, will be able to harm you if you wear Aphrodite's Girdle.

Lyre

As the attribute of Apollo in his more artistic mode, the Lyre betokens the true harmony that music can bring. As with the cithara, the number of strings on a lyre can vary from three to twelve, but the correct number for Apollo's instrument is seven, that number being sacred to him. Those of artistic inclination will naturally be drawn to this symbol. Its magical task is to effect the stimulation of artistic and creative gifts in the user so that, like Orpheus, he or she may walk the paths of

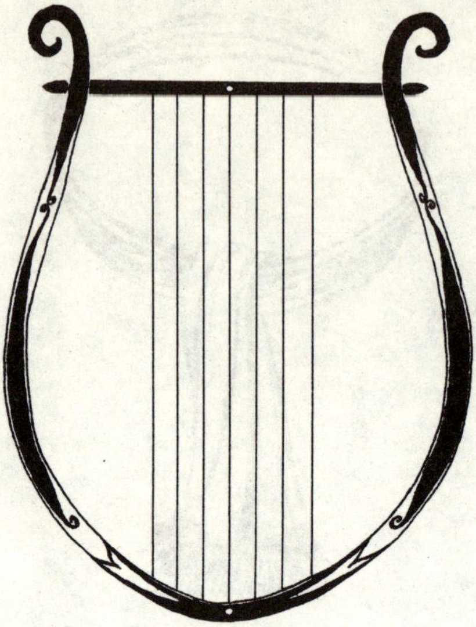

LYRE

altered states of consciousness in the safe knowledge that even the most horrendous of lower astral monsters will stand back and listen in awe to the sound of the music of the spheres. The way of beauty and gentleness is yet another safe method for negotiating the rock-strewn path to Olympus.

Flute

This most sacred of musical intruments was invented by Athene herself and is highly significant in the Greek magical system. There are several kinds of flute, the simple instrument illustrated here being the most familiar. Every living creature is imbued with a spark of the divine which carries a personal sonic or sound frequency. Legend has it that were this knowledge to become readily available it could be used either to kill or cure, so with our world in its present state it is perhaps better that we do not possess the key to the sonic code. However, there is nothing to prevent us making contact with our own personal sonic, and that of others, via the sounds of the flute. The Pan call was originally played on the flute in Atlantean times and the purity of its tone is said to encourage equally pure energies. If you, the aspiring Hero, are of musical inclination learn to play the flute and Athene

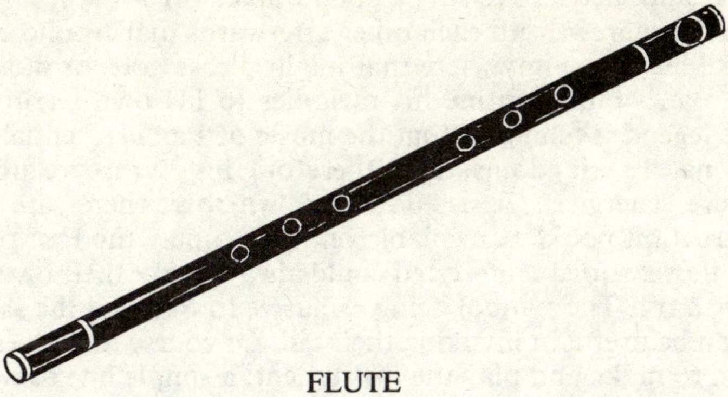

FLUTE

or Pan may well honour you with their presence.

Syrinx

While on the subject of musical instruments we might as well take into account Pan's Syrinx. The myth tells us that Pan pursued the chaste nymph Syrinx from Mount Lycaeum to the river Ladon where she turned herself into a reed to escape his embraces. As he was unable to distinguish her from the other reeds arrayed on the river bank, Pan cut several at random and made them into his famous pipe. Although basically a nature divinity, Pan was also drawn to music and the dance and on one occasion he jokingly dared to challenge the god of music himself to a contest. King Midas was the

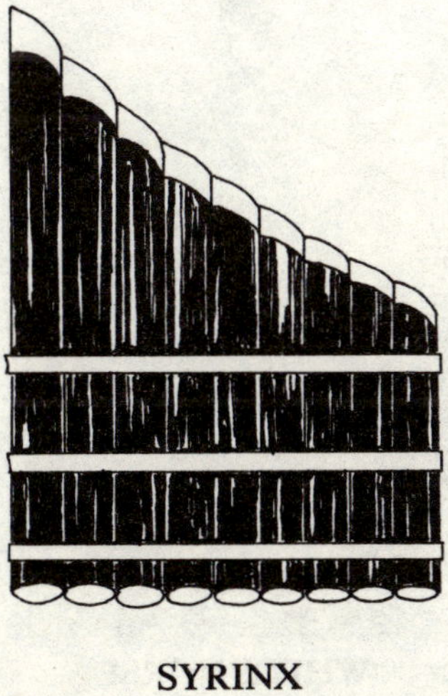

SYRINX

judge and, needless to say, Apollo walked off with the laurels. But they agreed with each other afterwards that Apollo could make his music anywhere that might please gods or mortals, but Pan would confine his melodies to his own territories. The legend is telling us that the music of Pan is essentially of the nature kingdoms, and therefore his Syrinx relates to nature energies. It is doubtful whether there are any instruction booklets available on how to play the Pan pipes, but those who are interested could always make their own and have a try. The symbol being exclusive to Pan and the satyrs, it can be useful in invoking their aid. Of course, one does not need to make and play the instrument; a simple line drawing, when meditated upon, will produce the desired effect.

White Horse

This was another Poseidon emblem and the Greeks were by no means the only people to employ the White Horse symbology. The reason for this is that it undoubtedly originated in the 'old country' (Atlantis) where the White Horse was highly revered towards the latter days, no doubt on account of the slowly rising waters whose ruling deity the

WHITE HORSE

priests wished to placate. In the Trismegistic teaching it is spoken of as representing purified passion and, in view of Poseidon's influence over the human emotions, this is easily understandable. Its marine associations being undeniable, the White Horse can be employed magically to rise above any tricky emotional situation on the one hand, or inner psychological conflict on the other.

Thyrsus

The ivy-twined, pine-cone-tipped staff is a potent magical symbol representing the Dionysian energies. These work through delusion which is, of course, a double-edged sword. Just as one can be beguiled into thinking that Dionysus, his tutor Silenus and their ribald band were a bunch of debauchees, so the aspiring Hero can employ this symbol to obscure his real identity. If you have earned the right to carry

THYRSUS

the Thyrsus — and only Dionysus can give you this once you have passed his stringent tests of self-discipline — you may deceive an enemy into thinking whatever you wish him to think about you, from seeing you as a highly powerful individual, to a nondescript man or woman not worth wasting his time or energy on. You can appear as a jolly, bright, friendly soul to those whom it so pleases you, or as a sombre scholar should that situation be more to your advantage. But, first of all, earn your Thyrsus and Dionysus and his satyrs will do the rest for you.

The Rainbow

This is, for the aspiring Hero, the symbol of hope. It should be used for meditation during the 'dark night of the soul', or 'abyss' through which every magical student must pass if he or she is eventually to attain to the Olympian heights. A representation of the Rainbow in any art form will always serve as a reminder that no condition or adversity is destined to last for ever.

THE RAINBOW

Helmet of Invisibility

This symbol is the attribute of Hades. Use it after the manner of the veil of Nephthys, the hidden one of Egyptian magic, to cloak yourself or remain unnoticed at times when you do not wish to draw attention to your person. Naturally, it

HELMET OF INVISIBILITY

constitutes an excellent emblem for protection both in and out of the body.

Sceptre Surmounted by a Cuckoo

The cuckoo, who lays her eggs in the nests of other birds, symbolizes either the arrival of a spirit or intelligence from a different evolutionary stream or the incarnation of a godling or hero. The accommodating foster-bird acts as a nurse to the alien whose own natural parents are unable to attend to such functions at an earthly level, their species having evolved beyond that point. Hercules was a perfect example of this. Born of an Olympian father to a mortal mother, his descent into matter suggests the god-conscious soul that needs to purge itself of its human weaknesses before it can claim its divinity. A normal birth to an earthly mother is, therefore, essential, for how otherwise can this soul know, feel and experience as a mortal? Zeus cuckolded Amphitryon and the sacred egg he deposited in Alcmene's nest quickly outgrew the smaller nestling and eventually developed the plumage necessary for its long flight back to its own kind.

The Sceptre is Hera's queenly symbol, while the Cuckoo is there to remind us that those exalted souls who choose to incarnate among us often select very ordinary environments into which to be born. They may well grow to stand head and shoulders above their siblings, but they are destined soon to leave the nest to be on their way and about their tasks. They are the souls who have individuated from the 'collective' so there is, therefore, no native nest here on Earth to which they may return.

SCEPTRE SURMOUNTED BY A CUCKOO

Hera's Sceptre may be used by those who feel themselves ready to negotiate the individuation break. Being the 'cuckoo in the nest', or the 'odd one out' will naturally cause resentment among others of the group, but with Hera's help the young bird may proceed safely on its flight without fear of hindrance or interference from its adopted family.

Thunderbolt

Although this is the attribute of the father of the gods, it is not the magical tool for everyone. It represents a specialized

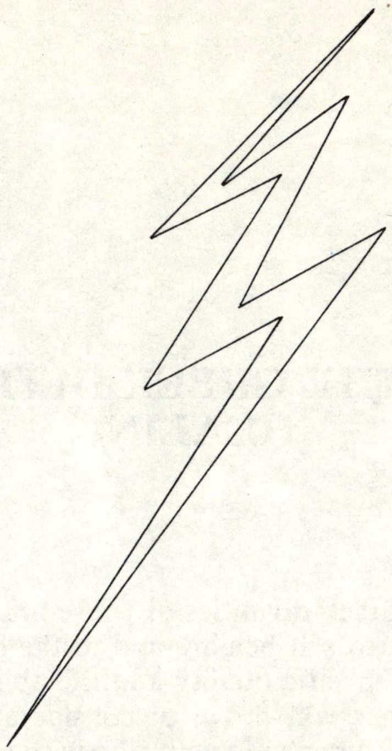

THUNDERBOLT

energy of a dissolving and reforming nature and Zeus only hurled it at those he wished to destroy or halt in their tracks. The Thunderbolt should not be used by the aspiring Hero unless it is given to him as a special present by Zeus himself, in which case its application should be confined to bringing down old spiritual edifices to make room for new and more expansive modes of cosmic consciousness.

*   *   *

These are the main magical symbols to be encountered in the Olympian system. There may be others that are private to the aspiring Hero, but these will be gifts from the tutelary deity either as rewards for bravery or in exchange for energies expended or services rendered to the god by the aspiring Hero. In which case keep them to yourself; they are not the concern of anyone except you, your chosen divinity and your magical tutor.

18. THE GREEK DEITIES OF HEALING

Several of the Greek divinities dispense healing rays that can be applied both to self-healing and to the healing of others. Each ray has a specific quality and the ability to distinguish one from another will prove of considerable help to those dedicated to the therapeutic path who wish to avail themselves of the healing forces of Olympus.

Hermes
God of practical or rational medicine, Hermes is the doctor's divinity. In other words, he can help your doctor, or those who are qualified by law to administer or practise medicine, to diagnose your condition correctly and apply the right treatment. He should, therefore, be invoked prior to visiting a hospital or your general practitioner. Hermes' energies can also help the individual to understand and respect the inner workings of his or her own body.

Pan
Son of Hermes, Pan's healing energies are quite different and more concerned with natural remedies. Floral, herbal and tree cures, folk medicine and Paracelsus's famous 'doctrine of signatures' are all areas covered by Pan's healing rays. Fevers are his speciality, also open ulcers or those stubborn physical wounds that defy normal healing applications. The next time you are suffering from influenza or a pyrexia (temperature)

ask him to help and, although your doctor may be surprised at your speedy recovery, you will know the truth behind it.

Apollo

Representing the solar power, the Apollonine healing rays are highly effective and can be applied to any bodily ailment. They work by stimulating or reactivating the body's own natural healing properties which have often been deadened by drugs or ill use of the physical vehicle over a period of years. Sunshine and fresh air were always known to help the convalescent, but during the inclemency of the northern winter many of us are unable to indulge in such luxuries, which is when a goodly dose of Apollo can help us.

Artemis

Artemis is the divinity of mental healing, the frequency or wave-length of her energies applying more to sickness of the mind than to physical maladies. The Egyptian masters equated her with their own cat goddess, Bast, who was also a healer of the mentally afflicted. Like the healing centaur, Chiron, she draws her power from the animal kingdoms and the Elements. The cat, as well as other animals sacred to Artemis, has for many years been known to carry mentally therapeutic energies. Her Bow and Arrow will help you to pinpoint the problem while her gentle animal friends will visit their healing energies on you, probably during sleep state.

Athene

As goddess of self-imposed discipline, Athene is the natural instructor in the art of self-healing. Her Spear can help to open up the subconscious mind and so allow any emotional blockages to rise to the surface. Those who would like to master the 'self' should seek the services of this wise goddess and, having learned to control their own bodies, they will be better equipped to help others to understand theirs.

* * *

Practitioners of alternative therapies may draw on any of the Olympian healing deities according to the nature of the complaint they are treating, although their ministrations are more likely to fall under the guidance of Pan, Apollo or

Artemis than Hermes or Athene. But no matter what the condition, there is a god, goddess or godling who can help out without interfering with your own karmic pattern or that of your patient.

19. THE TWELVE LABOURS OF HERCULES AND THEIR ESOTERIC MEANINGS

Many historians are of the opinion that to the early Greeks the heroes were no more or less than ancestors who were looked back upon with pride. Heroes and ancestors were offered sacrifice at the end of the day, the sacrificial victim was turned to the west and a trench dug at the foot of the altar to receive the head. But the chief role of the hero was, as we have already described, to act as an intermediary between man and gods, having himself achieved a sort of midway position between the Earth and Olympus.

To engage in an analysis of the deeds and adventures of all the heroes would take more time and space than this book allows and, besides, not all of the fables recounted carry occult connotations, so it will be up to the aspiring Hero, with the assistance of his or her tutor, to work out which is which.

One hero, probably the greatest, whose adventures do relate to the initiatory experience was Heracles, so-called because he was said to owe his fame to the machinations of Hera but later known as Hercules. The story goes that Zeus, wishing to have a son strong enough to protect both mortals and immortals, assumed the form of one Amphitryon in order to lie with that gentleman's wife, Alcmene, whom Zeus knew to be a direct descendant of the hero Perseus. Within a few days Amphitryon himself returned from the wars and also accommodated his spouse. From these successive unions Alcmene conceived two sons, Hercules and Iphicles.

Expecting his son to arrive on a given day, Zeus swore a solemn oath before all the Olympians that the descendant of Perseus who was about to be born should one day rule Greece. Upon hearing these words Hera was consumed with jealousy and sought to foil her husband's plan. Hastening to Thebes she deliberately retarded the birth of Hercules and arranged for the wife of one Sthnelus — also a son of Perseus — to give birth prematurely. Unable to break his word, Zeus was obliged to bestow the kingship on the first-born child, who was Eurystheus. Having placed her puppet firmly in authority over Hercules, Hera was able to ensure that the hero's life was made as difficult as possible.

There are many stories told of the strength and courage of the young Hercules, which we will leave for the student to read for him or herself. How he came to be saddled with the Labours is a long tale involving a period of madness that Hera had deliberately visited on him, during which he mistook his own children for enemies and slew them. After the realization of what he had done dawned on him, he consulted the Delphic oracle at whose suggestion he committed himself to twelve years in the service of Eurystheus.

As has already been explained, the number '12' is sacred to Greek magic and is very much a part of the magical philosophy of this planet. There are twelve signs of the Zodiac (and many believe there to be twelve planets in this solar system); twelve apostles; twelve knights of the Round Table, twelve months in the solar year, etc., so let us commence by saying that the number of Hercules' Labours and years of servitude is significant in itself. The details of the Herculean stories have obviously become confused over the centuries, all sorts of little extras being included to add emphasis to the great hero and what the people of those times considered to be 'strong man stuff'. So it is essential to take this into account.

One of the most popular explanations of the twelve Labours is that each task represents the lessons to be learned from the twelve signs of the Zodiac. The four-seasoned year has also been mentioned, as represented in Ezekiel's vision of the bull, lion, eagle and seraph or man, but from the occult standpoint a deeper analysis is called for.

The First Labour — The Nemean Lion

Using the quaternary symbology, the lion represents the Element of Fire. From a general assessment of the nature of Hercules himself, it would appear that the principles of this Element were dominant in his psyche, so it is only natural that his first occult encounter would be with that Element. Slaying the lion would mean coming to terms with the Element of Fire within himself. As most occultists know, the student always attracts the good offices of that Element which is strongest and most secure in his own psychology, so we are beginning to catch our first glimpses of the true nature of this archetypal hero.

Eurystheus had ordered Hercules to bring back the skin of the lion, probably as proof that the hero had actually disposed of the beast. Hercules obliged, but from the hide he fashioned an invulnerable garment, while the lion's head he made into a helmet. The myth is telling us that the Initiate needs to become as one with the lion, i.e. 'wear its skin and see through its eyes' as it were, in order to understand its strength and partake of the finer spiritual qualities it represents.

The Second Labour — The Lernaean Hydra

This creature was a marsh-dwelling, nine-headed serpent. Hercules sought to slay it with his club, but as fast as he severed one of the heads two more grew in its place. He was finally able to despatch it with the aid of Fire, having earned the right to draw on the energies of that Element as a result of his successful leonian encounter. So what can we learn from this? That sheer brute strength (the club) is no match for the cunning contrivances of the emotions and the only way to tackle the ever-rearing head of personal desire is to transmute its energies into the creative mode via the fiery experience.

The Third Labour — The Ceryneian Hind

Although Robert Graves names this as the third Labour, other authorities give the boar of Erymanthus as number three. However, for the purpose of this book we will stay with Graves. Far from being a nuisance factor, the Ceryneian hind was a creature of great beauty, speed and skill. Not wishing to wound or kill such a fine beast, Hercules hunted her untiringly for a whole year and finally caught her in a net (some say by pinning her forelegs together with an arrow without drawing blood). He was obliged to put things right with Artemis, however, since the hind was sacred to that goddess. But, once he explained the problem, Artemis was understanding and allowed him to leave her territories in peace.

Here we have a spiritual pursuit in which the hero seeks a prize of great rarity. The kingdoms of Artemis are the animal kingdoms on the one hand and the realms of the inner mind on the other. Hercules needed to learn that an animal can be a thing of beauty to be respected and cherished, that not all aspects of the 'self' are monsters to be destroyed, and that true might is only as strong as it is gentle!

The Fourth Labour — The Boar of Erymanthus

The boar itself presented no problems for Hercules who captured it alive, bound it with chains and carried it back across his shoulders. But another incident occurred during this little adventure that was of initiatory import. An arrow from the hero's bow accidentally struck his old friend, the centaur Chiron. Although Hercules attended to the wound under Chiron's skilled medical instructions, the pain was not eased and, being immortal, the centaur could not gain relief through death. So he offered his immortality to Prometheus, a gesture which greatly moved Zeus who thereupon placed Chiron's image in the stars as the constellation of Sagittarius.

In this Labour Hercules easily mastered the 'boar' within himself, but in the process he wounded a dear friend. The lesson is that although we may overcome certain boorish traits in our own character this does not give us power over life and death, the aspiring Hero being as vulnerable where the loss of a loved one is concerned as his weaker brother. Earth can oft-times be a valley of tears for even the strongest among us, especially when we find ourselves powerless to help those we love. But the gods forget neither us nor our loved ones, the memory of whom is written in the stars for ever!

The Fifth Labour — The Stables of Augeias

King Augeias possessed a fine herd of cattle, but their stabling had become so loaded with filth that the poor beasts were unable to rest comfortably therein. Moreover, the accumulation of the effluent was causing distress and disease in the surrounding countryside. Eurystheus assigned to Hercules the task of cleaning them out, gleefully relishing the thought of the hero's mortification at having to handle personally such a disgusting load. Hercules, however, had it all worked out and guaranteed to cleanse the whole area before nightfall. This he did by making two breaches in the wall of the yard and diverting the neighbouring rivers so that they flowed through the place, carrying all the dung with them and also cleansing the nearby pastures. Because the help of the river gods had been sought, Eurystheus refused to accept the cleansing of the stables as a task fulfilled, but in spite of this it is always recognized as one of Hercules' twelve Labours.

Here the Initiate is being shown how the most onerous of tasks can be handled with ease, with a little help from the denizens of other worlds, i.e. the Water elementals. Hercules' ingenuity was one thing, but without the co-operation of the river divinities he would have experienced considerable difficulty in fulfilling this Labour. Man is not the only intelligence in the universe and the sooner he realizes that his own inventiveness is not always to be relied upon he will, like Hercules, make a better job of cleaning up the mess he has made of his own planet.

The Sixth Labour — The Stymphalian Birds

A flock of brazen-winged, man-eating birds sacred to Ares had left their normal hunting grounds and taken up residence in the Stymphalian marsh, from where they attacked man and blighted crops. Hercules arrived at the marsh, but there were too many birds to despatch with his arrows, added to which the marsh was too soft to support his weight. Standing by the bank somewhat puzzled as to what to do next, Hercules was visited by Athene who made him a present of a pair of bronze castanets. When he shook these the noise was so terrifying that the birds rose in one great flock and fled from the spot, the hero felling several of them as they winged away to some far-off place where they could no longer prove a nuisance.

Bird symbology is usually employed to represent the ascent of the spirit, either to higher realms or simply out of the body. As the Stymphalian birds were of a destructive nature the warning is that all the manifestations the aspiring Hero is likely to encounter during altered states of consciousness are not benign. Because the ground Hercules stood upon was marshy, he was unable to use his normal defensive weaponry to full effect. The Initiate is therefore advised to earth himself firmly before taking on any out-of-the-body adversaries. Allowing the emotional nature, as depicted by the moisture of the swamp, to render him vulnerable could cost him the initiation. But, fortunately, there is always the tutelary deity to help out with the gift of a suitable magical symbol, although the aspiring Hero's ability to handle this will form part of the initiation. Athene obliged Hercules with a sonic device which served to drive the offending creatures of the air back to an environment more suited to their stage of evolutionary development. The modern aspiring Hero may find that many of the 'nasties' he or she encounters in other dimensions will also need to be handled in this way.

The Seventh Labour — The Cretan Bull

Although Eurystheus was reputed to have ordered Hercules to capture the Cretan bull, legend also has it that Zeus himself imposed this test upon his son. Hercules managed to catch the creature single-handed and after many trials he brought it back to Mycenae. There is a touch of Theseus and the minotaur about this episode which suggests that it probably originated in some earlier rite in which the initiate was obliged to engage in combat, either with a real bull or someone disguised as such. A ritual of this nature was also included in the Dionysian Mysteries at one particular stage. For the deeper meaning we must consider the intervention of Zeus himself and move the whole drama to a more esoteric level. This presents us with a picture of the hero being obliged to face up to and overcome a less desirable trait in his character, the nature of which was of particular concern to the father of the gods.

As a traditional symbol of the Element of Earth, the bull in this story would appear to allude to Hercules' tendency to be a shade too materialistic, a trap into which an Initiate may fall at any time when things appear to be going well for him or her.

The Eighth Labour — The Mares of Diomedes

For his eighth Labour, Hercules was ordered to capture the savage, flesh-eating mares of the Thracian king Diomedes.

With the aid of a few volunteers he succeeded in driving the beasts down to the sea, where he left them on a knoll. Although grossly outnumbered by the angry keepers who set out in pursuit, Hercules and his little band succeeded in overcoming them by once again courting the good offices of the elemental forces. Hastily digging a channel which allowed the sea to flood the low-lying plain, they cut their pursuers off and dealt with them appropriately. The mares eventually devoured the king himself and, their appetites being thus assuaged, they no longer constituted a nuisance factor.

In this Labour, our hero is exposed to the power of corrupt authority, that which feeds off the flesh of the people as it were. The beasts, representing the offending principle, are driven down to the sea, the traditional place of cleansing, with the perpetrators of the evil deeds in hot pursuit. The Element of Earth is the channel through which the cleansing and protecting waters may run, thus confining the enemy to one place wherein he is faced with the rebounding force of his own violence. The king's final destruction by his own mares tells the eternal tale of a contaminating force that is eventually devoured by the manifestations of its own corruption.

The Ninth Labour — Hippolyte's Girdle

Eurystheus's daughter, Admete, coveted the golden Girdle of Ares which was owned by Hippolyte, queen of the Amazons, so Hercules was duly despatched to obtain it for her. During the first part of his journey he was accompanied by several other celebrated heroes, notably Theseus, Telemon and Peleus, but upon reaching the country of the Amazons he was personally able to pursuade the queen to give him the Girdle as a gift. The ease of this quest annoyed Hera to such an extent that she assumed the disguise of one of the Amazonian warrior ladies and spread the story that Hercules was up to no good with their queen. As a result of this move the hero was forced to fight his way out of the situation. But in spite of this temporary inconvenience he secured the Girdle and brought it back for Admete.

The Girdle being a traditional symbol of binding, Hercules' ninth mission suggests that he was called upon to break the bonds by which his *anima* was held in the submissive mode as a result of the heroic role he had undertaken. Being ladies of masculine inclinations, the Amazons represented an overaccentuation of the *animus* in the female body. Admete was, it seems, another name for Athene, Hercules' own tutelary goddess, so it was for his tutelary divinity that he needed to obtain the Girdle. Hera's interference in Amazonian guise indicates the battle the hero must have experienced with his own *animus* prior to securing the Girdle for Athene and thereby passing the initiation.

No matter which role we may choose to adopt prior to incarnating in any one life, to grow spiritually we must always have an understanding of the parts played by others in the cosmic drama. In order to achieve this state of awareness it becomes necessary for us to subjugate our own egos by freeing them at will from their chosen stereotype. Hercules was essentially the strong, macho male — all *animus*. The Girdle, remember, was Aphrodite's attribute and therein lies the initiation.

The Tenth Labour — The Cattle of Geryon

Geryon was a triple-headed monster who reigned over the western coast of Iberia. He owned a herd of oxen that were safely guarded by his herdsman Eurytion and the dog Orthrus. As ordered by Eurystheus, Hercules overcame the herdsman and the dog and took possession of the oxen, undergoing several other minor tests while journeying to and from the place. On one occasion Hera sent a gadfly that stung the cattle, driving them mad so that they dispersed through the mountains causing Hercules considerable difficulty in catching them. While undertaking this Labour Hercules also visited Gaul, where he abolished human sacrifice.

Geryon's triple heads suggest the triple goddess, whose worship was strong in the Iberian regions. Hercules taking possession of the oxen no doubt alludes to the religion of his father, Zeus, assuming ascendency over the prevailing matriarchal cults. But the task would have been simpler for Hercules in the larger towns and cities than in the mountains where remnants of the old religion were still strong; hence Hera's dispersal of the cattle over those regions.

At the personal heroic level the Labour describes the aspiring Hero's quest through many schools of belief before he finally finds that which he feels to be right for him. And even then his faith can be shattered into fragments and dispersed over the wastelands of human experience. As a result of this lesson, the Initiate learns that there is a point at which sacrifice, either of the 'self' or others, ceases to become necessary and must, therefore, be abolished from spiritual thinking modes, there being no such thing as a required sacrifice in the final analysis — only experience.

The Eleventh Labour — The Apples of the Hesperides

Although Hercules had performed the first ten Labours in the space of eight years and one month, Eurystheus discounted the second and fifth on the grounds that the hero had received too much external aid and set him two more. The first of these involved fetching fruit from the golden apple tree that had been the wedding gift to Hera from the Earth herself. So pleased had Hera been with this gift that she planted it in her own personal garden. As with all mythological trees of this nature, an ever-vigilant dragon named Ladon was curled around it to protect the fruit from pilferers.

During this Labour Hercules encountered the usual series of obstacles including a giant whose strength was renewed each time his feet touched the Earth. The hero defeated the giant by holding him aloft in the air until his energies ran out. The prophet Nereus advised Hercules by which road he should travel and, needless to say, that very route was beset with every conceivable setback. In spite of this the hero performed several good deeds during the course of his journey, including slaying the eagle that constantly tortured Prometheus, which finally freed the old Titan from his purgatory. Hercules eventually reached the garden of the Hesperides where he despatched Ladon and took the Apples as Eurystheus had requested.

Another story has it that Atlas aided him in this quest by picking the Apples while Hercules held the world on his shoulders for the giant. Atlas, however, was as reluctant to hand over the delicious fruit as he was to take back his traditional burden. By following advice Nereus had previously given him, however, the hero was able to outwit the giant.

The Hesperides were the four children of Atlas and Hesperis. Their abode was beyond the river-ocean at the extreme western limits of the world and they were said to be personifications of the clouds illuminated by the rays of the setting Sun. In other words, the Hesperides gardens were a sort of retiring summerland of great beauty and a spot beloved of the gods. Apples represent a kind of forbidden fruit but not, in this instance, of the Adam and Eve variety.

Hercules was nearing the end of his trials by reaching a place so blessed. But although the fruits of his Labours were within sight and touch, they were still not his for the taking; they had to be rendered justly to another. Eurystheus gave them to Athene, who returned them to the nymphs, as it was against Olympian Law for Hera's property to pass out of their hands. Esoterically, the apples are indicative of the joys to come, which the aspiring Hero is permitted to glimpse, but which must then be returned to their rightful sphere. The tree is the Qabalistic Tree of Life, or the Norse Yggdrasil, which the Hero must eventually come to know if he is to comprehend the nature of life. The help rendered by the prophetic divinity, Nereus, is also significant, the tutor always ensuring that the right advice is communicated to his pupil in one way or another. By freeing Prometheus from his suffering, Hercules made the Titan's services once more available to mankind while the Atlas episode suggests that there will be times when humanity will try to foist the weight of the world onto the shoulders of the aspiring Hero but, as the legend tells us, that is *not* his role and he must not, therefore, allow himself to become saddled in this way.

The Twelfth Labour — The Capture of Cerberus

The last and probably the most difficult Labour allotted to Hercules was to bring Cerberus up from Tartarus. He prepared for this task by presenting himself for initiation at the Eleusinian Mysteries and seeking the aid of Hermes, the divine patron of travellers. Hercules underwent many adventures on this perilous journey but, after wounding Hades, Hercules received the lord of the Underworld's permission to carry off Cerberus, the proviso being that no weapons were to be used. It was in this final feat that Hercules really came into his own as he was able to make the best use of his great strength. He overpowered and brought back Cerberus to Eurystheus, after which he freed the beast so that it could return to its own dark domains. In other words, the hero had finally overcome death itself by showing no fear of its terrors. No longer did the lower regions have power over him.

One day, after the gods had deemed that Hercules had been sufficiently tested, the hero felt consumed by an inner fire the pain of which became so intense that he believed his end had finally come. Preparing his own funeral pyre in the hope of escaping into death, he begged his companions to set light to it. They all refused except Poeas, father of Piloctetes, who lighted the pines, whereupon the hero made him a parting present of his bow and arrows. But that was not the end. As the flames rose and Hercules prepared himself fearlessly to meet his end, a cloud descended from the skies, thunder and lightning shook the Earth and Zeus came to claim the spirit of his son for immortality.

The phenomenon of thunder and lightning is said to proclaim the passing of the souls of the just, recognized holy books quoting many examples. But organized religion does not, of course, hold the prerogative of sanctity as similar occurrences have taken place at the death of other noted adepts, Carl Jung being one example. As Fire is the senior Element, it is only fitting that the Salamanders should undertake the first stages of refining the ascending spirit to a point at which it can negotiate the realms beyond physical matter with facility and spiritual purity.

* * *

These twelve Labours of Hercules simply serve as guides to the Initiate and are not indications of the type of problems likely to be encountered by every aspirant. The monsters that constituted trials for Hercules might well present no difficulties whatsoever for the student of the Olympian Path who reads and chooses to assimilate the teachings in this book. What each of us is faced with and how we cope is a very individual thing; there can be no hard and fast rules. In fact, the very nature of Greek magic is against compartmentalization. The Initiate is encouraged to step forth and seek his or her own 'monsters' to slay, people to help, treasures to win and spiritual goals to attain. The universe is your initiation chamber, aspiring Hero or Heroine, and the book of rules is written within your own conscience. Hercules may have erected a few signposts, but time and evolution have long since worn their markings away. When confronted by the crossroads of experience the choice will be yours and yours alone!

20. INVOCATION, EVOCATION AND SECRET RITES

Those who feel drawn to ritual magic will naturally enquire as to how this is accommodated within the Greek system. Let us first establish that Olympian magic can be used with or without ritual, ceremony not being an essential prerequisite to its effectiveness. What really counts is the aspiring Hero's strength of mind and ability to adapt to whatever situation he finds himself faced with at any given time.

But, for the ritualists, here are a few tips on magical procedures. First of all it is important to realize that the Heroic Path is a lone one and *does not* demand the group experience. So, aspiring Hero, you may work entirely alone but, should you wish to include others, it must be on the strict understanding that it is *you* and not *they* who are initiating. Each man or woman must eventually go solo, accompanied only by his or her tutor and chosen deity.

An altar can be a good thing, as it serves as a focal point for the consciousness, which helps to counteract the stressful conditions of materialistic life. Construct your altar and dedicate it to your tutelary deity, using the appropriate colours and symbols, plus any additions that might be advised by your tutor. You should also include in the layout that personal emblem which your god will give you at a certain point in your Olympian travels. This you may not have in the early stages, but no matter. Study the chapter on symbols carefully and add any which you feel apply particularly to you as an individual. There is a symbol or emblem to cover most contingencies, any outstanding deficiencies in this area being quickly taken care of by the tutor or guiding god-form.

The quaternary principle, as represented by the Elements of Fire, Air, Earth and Water, should be acknowledged in all magical workings. When invoking the Elements, make use of the Greek names for the four winds (see Chapter 5) and address these personally when facing the four cardinal points of the compass.

Workings may follow standard magical procedures commencing with cleansing and mental preparation. The protective invocations should then follow before the Elements are called in. The principal deity presiding should always be the tutelary god or goddess and it will be up to him or her, and not to you, as to whether another god-form, godling, or magical beast is invited to enter the circle of protection. *THIS IS IMPORTANT!* In Greek magic the aspiring Hero *requests* the presence of the god. He does *not* command, nor at any time does he assume the god-form! Individuality is the keynote, tempered by both intuition and logic.

Having attended to the preliminaries, paid due deference to the tutelary divinity and humbly invited his or her presence, the heart of the ritual may be commenced. This could involve a specific request, either for help or wisdom, assistance in some earthly good deed, such as the promotion of harmony, peace or healing, or simply an affirmation of faith or love. Should some special area of help be required which is not normally covered by the tutelary god or goddess, then a fellow Olympian of appropriate calling will be brought in. Let us say, for example, that the tutelary deity is Demeter, but assistance has been requested to find a lost animal. Demeter will most certainly call in Artemis to help. Or perhaps Zeus is presiding over the ceremony and healing is desperately needed for someone close. The father of the gods will instruct Hermes to officiate, or perhaps the centaur Chiron whose healing skills also cured both gods and men.

Having completed your dialogue with the gods, thanks are in order all round and a prayer of gratitude should be offered to the gods, godlings, fabulous beasts, elementals and nature divinites who might have participated in the procedures and rendered their help. All ritual workings must be carefully closed and those forces that have been invoked returned to their rightful sphere of operation. Specialized energies which have been requested *must be used*! Should circumstances prevent this, they need to be returned to their place of origin with a request to the being or divinity involved to utilize them in some way appropriate to the relief of suffering here on Earth. It is of no use invoking a ray and then deciding it is not needed, so when in doubt seek your tutor's advice.

We do not intend to render a step-by-step guide to constructing a ritual working for Greek magic. As has already been emphatically stated, ceremony is *not* essential. If the aspiring Hero at some stage feels the need to employ its use, then he or she must draw on his or her own creative powers, or request instruction from his or her tutor as to how to handle the matter. Better, by far, is the use of mind magic in the Greek system as this does not limit one's activities to the ceremonial arena. And, after all, how many of the heroes of the past met their beasts of combat in a temple or sacred place. The truth was that, like Hercules they were obliged to sally forth to some unfamiliar clime, seek out the monsters and return with proof of their success. There are plenty of books which supply details as to how to invoke the Elements, etc., *Practical Egyptian Magic* being one of them.

On many occasions in this book it has been stated that information or instructions will be received from the tutor or the gods. As the aspiring Hero has also been advised always to balance intuition with logic, the question might well arise as to how this information is likely to be made available?

Greek magic functions in a perfectly natural way; bumps in the night, visits to mediums and spooky phenomena are not part and parcel of its scene. There is an interesting story recounted by Callimachus concerning an aspiring philosopher who sought the advice of Pittacos of Mytilene, one of the seven sages of Greece, regarding the choice of a wife. The question was whether he should marry a girl from his own class in society or seek to better himself with a nobler and wealthier partner. But Pittacos, rather than being specific in his reply, referred his client to a small group of children who were playing in the street outside, saying: 'See them. They will teach you what you should do.' Greatly disgruntled at what he took to be a total lack of help, the dissatisfied customer went his way. As he approached the children, who were deeply engrossed in their play, he heard one of them call out:

'Keep in line!' which immediately registered with him as an indication that he should not marry for money and position. Following this advice he was able to find true nuptial happiness and rise in life through his own talents and efforts.

The lesson to be learned from the aforegoing is that any advice deemed necessary for our magical education will be given in a very natural way via the everyday circumstances of life. For example, a book may fall open at a certain page while one is searching for something else; the TV set, irritatingly tuned to the wrong channel, may catch the very phrase that supplies the solution to a current problem; an unsolicited caller at the door or greetings between strangers in some public place could equally supply that much needed answer. Of course, it would be unbalanced to go through life suspecting that every overheard conversation contains some deeply esoteric message which, of course, is where a goodly dose of the old Greek logic enters the picture. All that can be said is that when a real message is delivered the aspiring Hero *will know*!

Another avenue through which the immortals may manifest is that of dreams. The symbology of dreams is highly complex, but to the person who is on the Heroic Path those nightly experiences will take on a new meaning and should be interpreted according to the symbology of the Greek school or tradition. It was Nietzche who commented, 'In our dreams, some archaic relic of humanity is at work,' and the Olympian system certainly provides a magical junction at which several earlier cultures, both primitive and highly advanced, come together. In the dream state we may contact the pre-conscious, as well as the sub-conscious and the super-conscious, which gives us access to our basic cosmic roots as well as the very essence of our beingness. This raw, spiritual canvas will in time become daubed with the colours of experience, and the aspiring Greek Hero will find the Hellenistic hues very much to his or her liking.

A question that is bound to arise is: 'As it is some centuries since the religion of Olympus was practised, surely the old god forms have now ceased to exist, or at least lost their powers?' During man's journey through the evolutionary cycle we term 'the material' he may change his beliefs many times, on each occasion clothing the new faith in the moral, spiritual and economically expedient fashion of the times. A flower that grows only in one clime still continues to exist and the fact that it may be unheard of in other regions neither diminishes its significance nor alters its pristine beauty. Much as it might wound his ego to know, man did *not* create the gods; they were always there and always will be! It matters little to them in what guise men choose to accept them or whether, in fact, they acknowledge their existence at all. Sooner or later the wheel will turn to complete yet another circle and a new generation of men will once again acknowledge and pay fealty to them.

Unlike the Egyptian magical tradition, the Greek system is very much of this planet. Agreed, there are certain cosmic overtones that it inherited from its Atlantean predecessors, but its own particular flavour is of *this* star-sun and its planetary children, especially the third one from the centre! Which goes to make Olympian magic the ideal vehicle for the magically-orientated member of the race of *Homo sapiens* to use for his or her ascent to the blessed heights.

21. RECONSTRUCTING THE ANCIENT ORACLES

Since it has already been stated that the Greek oracles of old were closely associated with ley-lines, power centres, chakras, or places of terrestrial emphasis, many of which would now appear to lie dormant, how could it be possible to bring the old oracles back to life?

The ancient Greeks, like other primitive peoples of their times, lived very close to nature and were, therefore, familiar with her pattern of working. They were more than aware of the fact that Mother Earth tended to surface her energies at given places, so what better than to use such sites to build temples or construct oracles? But all points of surfacing did not carry energies of exactly the same nature, as Mother Earth had many facets to her personality. Some of these facets were contributive to the art of learning, others to the powers of healing, and others to husbandry or the growth of plenty. So it was the task of the priest, shaman or wise woman to determine which was which. The construction appropriate to the nature of the energy could then be erected at the rightful place.

Whereas an educational establishment would be more suited to a site where the energies were more conducive to left hemisphere logic, oracles sprang up at points where the Earth energies served to stimulate the psychic faculty or workings of the right hemisphere of the brain. Such locations are by no means confined to the Hellenes. The first thing the aspiring

Hero, or anyone else interested in constructing their own Greek oracle, should do is to seek out a power centre, or crossing point for ley-lines where the energy generated by the junction activates the E.S.P. faculty. How is such a place to be found? For the aspiring Hero this will constitute an initiation; for the layman, a lesson in 'awareness'.

Once a suitable spot has been located, assuming of course that it does not involve trespassing or breaking the laws of the land (Zeus, remember, was a great one for upholding law and order, and he would be most displeased if such an action were to be carried out in his name or the names of his fellow immortals), a magical 'opening' and 'holding' procedure must be carried out. For this purpose ritual may be employed if it so suits the seeker but, again, it is not essential. The place must first be occultly cleansed of all previous associations and then opened up in the name of the chosen oracular deity. Let us say this is Apollo, patron of oracles. The aid of the Muses should first be sought and Apollo's sister also invited as good etiquette. Finally, a request should be addressed to the god himself to honour the spot with his presence.

The aspiring Hero can make direct telepathic contact with Apollo, or he may employ his own, private Pythia. *Warning*: do *not* make this into a group experience! People may be allowed to consult the oracle one at a time, but Apollo is not attracted to crowds, his energies being of a refined, artistic and delicate nature. Nor is it necessary to indulge in any form of false stimulation in order to make contact with the Greek god forces. Any experimentation with drugs or alcohol will only end in disaster, as it will be the lower nature of the user that will manifest in wild beast form and *not* the god himself, in which case any prophetic utterances will be far from accurate.

Once the oracle has been established the Net of Hephaestus should be used to hold it. Do not forget that if you wish to employ Hephaestian energies it is polite to request permission of the god and not take his co-operation for granted. He may, in fact, advise you in some way against the action and direct you to a spot better suited to your needs. Emergencies are bound to occur in life when the aspiring Hero will have to use the Net quickly, in which case a 'thank you' to Hephaestus after the event, plus a logical explanation of your actions, will not go amiss.

The serious student of Greek magic could derive considerable enlightenment from a properly constructed oracle for, as well as giving a voice to the higher powers, he or she will aid his or her own spiritual ascent and bring comfort, joy and happiness to mortals and immortals alike.

22. NEGATIVE FORCES AND HOW TO COMBAT THEM

The magical or occult path is never entirely free from negative encounters. By its very nature it cannot be, as the pursuit of knowledge and enlightenment inevitably opens up as many dark cupboards as it reveals truths of beauty and love. The higher you ascend up the Olympian mountain the greater will be your view of the countryside below. A mistaken and totally illogical impression so often received by aspirants to the occult path is that spiritual ascent is all roses, hymns and bright lights. The view from any height will expose all that is below it, verdant pastures and the gas works included; so a lesson in the realities of existence at all levels is essential in the early stages of occult development. A wise sage once likened steps taken along the initiatory path to 'looking for a gas leak with a lighted match'. In other words, occult energies tend to emphasize any deficiency in our make-up or personality. We all have our Achilles' heel, do we not? So we are back to 'Man, know thyself'.

The Greeks employed emphatic imagery to portray their 'nasties': fire-breathing monsters, red in tooth and claw, with numerous heads and serpents for hair, roamed the lands in search of prey. The exact location of these 'lands' was not always specified, however. Sometimes they were given as actual geographical locations, while in other instances we are presented with a picture of realms less physical wherein both gods and men were wont to wander. Occult 'nasties' fall into four main categories:

1. Those that are purely manifestations of the viewer's id, or some less desirable aspect of his or her lower self.

2. Separate entities in their own right that assume a horrendous appearance because they are young in evolution and know no better.

3. Deliberately malign intelligences whose ploy is to instil fear into the beholder.

4. Phantasms deliberately generated by the mind of another person of suspect intent, these being termed 'artificial elementals'.

The common denominator shared by all of the above is that they can be despatched, dispersed or disintegrated by the power of the mind. In other words, they can only exist if they are allowed to, the very act of fearing them serving to generate the sort of energies upon which they feed. One is reminded of Alice's ordeals with the aggressive queens: after she had put up with just so much of their tantrums the truth dawned on her, evoking her famous statement: 'You're only a pack of cards!'; whereupon they immediately collapsed because they were just that. Without her belief in their power to assume individual identities they were simply pieces of printed paper.

The 'bogies' of the Greek tradition are no more or no less than the opposing energies of any other system that may choose to show themselves in some childishly grotesque fashion. Logic is a good ally to have by one during any chance encounter of the less desirable kind, not that a little occult know-how doesn't help, mind you! Faith in oneself and one's own basic integrity is another powerful, personal defensive weapon and, of course, respect for the wisdom of the tutelary deity who probably arranged the encounter in the first place as a test.

Of course, the 'nasties' strewn across the path of the aspiring Hero will not always be ethereal ones. As the old Chinese proverb tells us: 'Destined enemies always meet in narrow passages', so opposition may well come from one's fellow men. Avoid the mistake of setting about the upward climb with any firm ideas as to what problems you are likely to be confronted with because, as sure as eggs are eggs, the gods will go out of their way to ensure that the ghouls you expect never materialize, but what does make its awesome appearance will take you completely and utterly by surprise.

Taking all things into account, ritual protection is *not* advised for the aspiring Hero. His weapons should always be with him and not in a box under the bed, or in some locked cupboard. His personal armoury should include the following:

1. His own intuition.
2. The symbol that connects him with his tutelary divinity.
3. The gift given to him personally by that deity.
4. Faith in himself and trust in those who guide him.
5. The resilience to pick himself up quickly after the inevitable falls.
6. The logic to use his intuition in a wise and balanced way.
7. A reliable psychic compass whose 'magnetic north' is Olympus.

Many traps into which the would-be Hero falls will be of his or her own making, however, and not the dire deeds of some opposing force. Everything can be overdone; logic, for example, which for all its positive uses also has its pitfalls. One is reminded of the true story of the atheistic humanist who, upon being confronted with a very emphatic spectral manifestation, declared that as there was no such thing he must be mentally sick and promptly confined himself to an institution. Strap hanging on what might appear to be secure, orthodox thinking modes can prove highly restrictive and can be just as responsible for mental breakdown or 'madness' as rebellious eccentricity or psychedelia. On the other hand, the rejection of convention for its own sake, without thought as to its ethical validity, is equally stupid. All in all, the safest way of dealing with the phantasms, egocentricities and insecurities of one's own mind is to keep it well disciplined, but always open to suggestions and advice.

The Heroic Path being a lone one, what advice is there for the Initiate who does find himself (or herself) faced with some unwholesome apparition which might appear to be getting the better of him?

Fear is the Initiate's worst enemy; mind-power is his ally. In the non-material worlds the mind rules, which means that whoever has the strongest thoughts is the boss of the situation. During that part of initiation designated 'the dark night of the soul', the worst possible fears raise their nasty heads. The slimy, gory monster of a bad dream has obviously been coped with if the dreamer wakes up — albeit in a sweat! But the gorgons of the abyss are within the 'self' and constitute whatever hurts the most. This will obviously vary with every individual. Some people are mentally overpowered by material worries, loss of job, money, status, etc.; while to others these values are of no concern. There are those who might rejoice in the expression of a specialized skill or art form of which, to their horror, some impending incapacity threatens to deprive them. Stress is always relative and initiation is — let's face it — stressful!

In that case, you may argue, everyone is undergoing initiation to a degree. This is indeed so, but the emphasis must be on the word 'degree'. Many a so-termed 'average' person (not that there is really any such thing, but may we be permitted to employ this term to distinguish between those who are on the Path and those who are not?) rushes to his or her doctor for tranquillizers after a couple of bad nightmares, or some slight but accidental encounter with an altered state of consciousness.

But such trivialities are nothing compared with the mind-blowing sequences that erupt as the psyche is stretched to the limits of its endurance during such heightened states of receptivity as may be experienced by the lone, aspiring Hero! He or she who would ascend the heights to immortality walks alone. Many helping hands may be extended along the journey, many friends made, many loves found and lost, and many tears shed. The gods will always fulfil their side of the bargain in some natural way, somebody's kind offices proving one of the many vehicles they are likely to employ. The tasks will be exacting and the 'monsters' many. There will be no one to take up arms on your behalf, only your tutor to tell you how to tackle the problem and which weapons to use and, if you do not possess those weapons in your armoury, then the god or goddess who watches over you will see that you are supplied with them in the nick of time. Once more a divine hand will stretch forth to move his or her piece on the Olympian chessboard, and an aspiring Hero or Heroine will have achieved yet another successful 'labour'.

23. CHOOSING THE HEROIC ROLE

Let us assume that having read this book the idea of the Heroic Path appeals to you. Your circumstances may be such that you have no one with whom to share the mystical experience, or perhaps you are a loner anyway and prefer it that way. But you have taken into consideration all the pros and cons and feel that you possess the kind of mentality that could accommodate the role of Hero.

How then does one get started? Not all of us are gifted with a highly creative imagination and, although one Initiate may not walk in the shoes of another, there are reliable signposts to point him in the right direction.

Having read and thoroughly digested your Greek mythology you will be familiar with the fact that there were numerous heroes, some better known and more highly respected than others. This illustrious band is bound to include many who were actually rulers, or men of renown whose deeds of valour left a strong imprint on the people of their time. But there are those special few who carry the pure archetypal quality which distinguishes them from the normal run of warriors and princes, causing them to stand out like beacons of light on the storm battered rocks of life. Hercules was just such a hero, so also were Perseus, Theseus and Odysseus. Take a deeper look into the esoteric significance of these four and you will observe a quaternary pattern emerging which allies their temperaments with the qualities of the four elements:

Hercules	—	Fire
Perseus	—	Air
Odysseus	—	Water
Theseus	—	Earth

Now for the next step. Look carefully into your own nature, strip aside any false *personae* and see if you really know yourself. Are you basically creative, intellectual, emotional, or practical! All right, so you feel yourself to be a very down-to-earth and solid sort of soul; then take the heroic name of Theseus. Or perhaps you belong to the 'up-and-at-'em' brigade, all action and ingenuity, in which case Hercules is your man. Remember, however, that there are two sides to every coin and although the positive attributes of an Element might be obvious in the psyche, the negative traits will also be present, as may be evidenced in Hercules' spell of insanity. But if, like Hercules, you possess the right heroic qualities you will eventually be able to reverse the coin again and correct any wrongs that were committed during the periods when your resistance was at a low ebb.

Choose your heroic name from those mentioned if you wish or, should you feel drawn to one of the other heroes of the classics, then borrow his nomenclature; he won't mind! If he really did exist he'll be gratified and, if he was only the figment of someone's imagination, then his literary creator has made a fine job of conveying an archetypal message that has evoked a legitimate response in you.

Having thus established your heroic identity, your quest must then be stirred into motion by your own mind. This will *not* involve a frenetic search into every conceivable altered state of consciousness (ASC) that can be practised. All it calls for is a quiet mental pursuit of the objective that will require no more than a short meditation each day, plenty of Greek reading matter to help tune you into the ethos, and a deep inner desire to succeed. Carry on with your day-to-day life and wait for the next step to unfold. If you find yourself growing impatient, send a telepathic message to your chosen divinity to ask why. Your first fault that comes up for correction may be impatience, and if you are unable to overcome this you may never start your journey in the first place. But the odds are that you will receive your instruction through some perfectly normal occurrence and your tutelary god or goddess will make his or her presence felt, most probably while you are studying or reading. Dream contacts with tutors and tutelaries are not always brought to consciousness on the following morning. One adept of the Olympian Path known to us beseeched the guiding divinity to show herself in a dream that night. The following morning, much to her disappointment, there was no recollection of a visitation. But half-way through the day, while she was engaged in some mundane task, the full realization of the nature of the goddess dawned on her and she knew that her request had been granted.

An anxious young person who had only been studying occult matters for a short period once put the question: 'When, oh when, will there be an end to this dreadful initiation that I seem to be going through?' The answer had to be, of course, 'Never'. Well, not in the way that she envisaged, because one initiation inevitably follows another all through life. Initiation is not like taking an examination, anxiously awaiting the results and then celebrating the victory (or drowning one's sorrows, as the case may be), after which a long, comfortable run of comparative calm ensues. With every test passed or 'labour' achieved one gains in strength and readiness for the next. Do they ever get easier? No. But each successive effort increases the command over the 'self', which gives one more power to cope. Life's problems can also be simplified if one can view them in a broader and more lucid perspective, such as can be achieved through a good magical discipline.

Try to consider initiation in this way: any course of magical study or pursuit results in an expansion of consciousness which slowly opens the mind and exposes the psyche to a wider vista of the universe. Never think of passing an initiation as rising or ascending to some higher and therefore more exalted plane. The expansion which does, in fact, take place is multi-directional and involves the whole of time and space.

Having arrived at this new level of awareness, the mind is presented with a fount of revolutionary concepts and eventualities that it is required to compute, rationalize and place into perspective. It is when the mind or psyche is unable to come to terms with this panorama and the seeker is obliged to retreat to the safety of his or her former beliefs that the initiation has been failed. Passing an initiation is no more or less than coping with a new set of spiritual or cosmic data, which means understanding it and feeling comfortable with it.

If you fall into the category of those who are forced to retreat to a former and more secure level of belief, then fair enough. There is no shame in that. Every man and woman must stay with what he or she feels to be right and the Heroic Path may not be destined for you this time around.

The Olympian pantheon is anything but chauvinistic, there being an equal number of gods and goddesses represented therein and, although Zeus is referred to as the father of the gods, Hera is also the mother of the gods. Nor was Zeus all-powerful in every avenue of endeavour. Athene was his master in battle and Aphrodite could always divert his shafts. So there is no distinction between male and female on the Heroic Path. But for ease in writing and presentation we have tended to use 'Hero' more than 'Heroine' and avoided as many 'he/shes' and 'his/hers' as possible. It should be taken as said, however, that all references to the aspiring Hero throughout this book apply to both male and female aspirants; please accept our apologies if the neglect of the continual use of the feminine gives offence. The goddesses seem quite happy about it all, anyway, and as long as their good offices are sought equally with those of the gods the balance is maintained.

With anyone on the Heroic Path, of course, a lot will depend on whether they are seeking to accentuate the *anima* or *animus* in this present time zone (life). The man who wishes to evoke an *anima* response in himself may well choose to serve Demeter, Aphrodite or Hera, while the woman who feels that her ineffectuality is due to a lack of *animus* may feel drawn to Ares, Zeus or Hephaestus. The main thing is that one does not develop a fixation about sexual roles, as this in itself can cause an imbalance that will only serve to delay the heroic journey or even halt it in its tracks.

24. SOME PRACTICAL ADVICE AND SUGGESTIONS

For the sake of safety-first, if nothing else, a few boring 'dos' and 'don'ts' are an essential inclusion in any work on magic. There are laws to be observed, painful though this statement may be to the more hedonistic among us, so let us take a look at the Greek or Olympian book of rules.

According to the nature of the ethos in which it developed, Greek magic is logical, democratic, lawful and disciplined. Zeus always punished the law breakers, whether they were mortals or immortals. This does not mean, of course, that some dark-bearded omnipotent being of Hellenistic appearance, armed with a bolt of lightning, sits perched on a mountain top from where he dispenses rude justice upon anyone who steps on his immortal corns! Zeus represents a principle which, in turn, corresponds to a cosmic law. The miscreant who finds himself or herself in the presence of the father of the gods is simply facing the 'Zeus' or lawgiver within him or herself, nothing more sinister. We are each the judge of our own destiny and, in the final analysis, it is the god within us, or that aspect of immortality which each and every one of us carries, that pronounces the judgments and dispenses the punishments. Modern techniques in hypnotherapy have served to confirm this truth. People suffering in one way or another, when subjected to deep trance state and questioned as to why they have accepted such a heavy or tragic burden have been known to reply to the effect that they made the choice in order to atone for former wrongs: the wheel of Karma, in other words.

But karmic debts can always be transmuted in service or through the realization of why one is suffering. Freud and his contemporaries scratched the surface of this truth in the discovery that the traumas of childhood can produce imbalances of mind and body during the mature years. Apply this principle to the karmic framework of the individual in *gestalt* and the answers become readily apparent.

Next point. How can a system of occult progress possibly qualify as democratic? Surely the occult is, by its very nature, undemocratic in that one does not become an adept by being voted in. True, of course, the magus is not required to court the votes of the populace in order to ascend the Olympian or any other magical heights. Democracy, in the case of Olympian magic, lies with the aspiring Hero's right to choose, the deity's right to refuse, and the tutor's right to teach only those whom it pleases him to so do. Of course, the aspiring Hero does stand to make a wrong decision, which could result either in no help at all being forthcoming, or an inappropriate energy being released which could make matters worse and not better.

An analogy springs to mind of a healing case involving a lady who suffered from spasmodic violent outbursts. The healers who had been working on her up to the point at which occult help was sought had been pumping energy into her for all they were worth. The good intentions and love were there, but the hoped-for results were not forthcoming and they were confused. Perceiving that the problem was due not to the body's lack of energy but to its manufacturing an excess of it the consultant occultist drew away the overflow and rebalanced the psychic and physical mechanisms that were causing the outbursts, whereupon the lady was cured. So it sometimes pays to know what to call upon and when.

The question that will inevitably arise from the above true story is why, if it is supposed to be all powerful, love did not prevail? A broken leg needs to be set; a poisoned arm needs to have the offending substances drawn out; an accident victim needs his or her open wounds attended to; and the sick mind needs professional adjustment. Love can certainly aid recovery in each case and, if its cosmic principle is embraced by the sufferer, it will help to ensure that they do not incur further damaging injury. The secret of the love power lies within each and every one of us. If we develop and nurture that principle it will manifest in our lives. As with any other gift from the gods, however, it will *not* guarantee us freedom from life's problems and ills. An occultist of repute once stated that if God were to reverse the Law of Gravity to stop one suicide taking his life, what would happen to the rest of the people on the planet? In other words, each level of creation is subject to a set of cosmic laws that are appropriate to the experience it has to offer to an evolving soul; to bend those rules to suit any one person would completely upset the lives of the other millions who rely on them for the furtherance of their spiritual aims and the fulfilment of their Karma.

One could go on philosophizing, so there must be a point at which the verbiage ceases and the conclusions are drawn. The Greek or Olympian Heroic Path is unique in that it opens the way for the lone traveller. This does not preclude the aspiring Hero from establishing friendships; in fact, it encourages him or her to do so, but respectfully requests that these associations be chosen from all orders of existence and not limited to *Homo sapiens*.

Did we say it was a 'lone' path? We take that back. Olympian magic opens up the doors to so many new areas of universal consciousness that the Initiate will find his psychic and intellectual senses confronted with a panorama of visionary experiences and logical answers that will never cease to amaze; and the inhabitants of those new worlds will be ever ready to accompany the aspiring Olympian and offer him or her every possible aid in the search for divinity.

So, dear Hero or Heroine, proceed on your way . . . and may the gods go with you.

BIBLIOGRAPHY

Atlantis and the Giants Denis Saurat (Faber & Faber, 1957).
Who Was St George? Bob Stewart (Moonraker Press).
The Symbolic Quest Edward Whitmont (Putnam & Sons, New York, 1969).
Astrology and Religion Among the Greeks and Romans Franz Cumont (Dover Publications, Inc. New York, 1960).
The Modern Textbook of Astrology Margaret E. Hone (C. N. Fowler, 1975 14th Edition).
The Spear of Destiny Trevor Ravenscroft (Thorsons Publishing Group, 1973).
Greek Oracles Robert Flaceliere (Paul Elek Ltd. St Albans, 1965).
Practical Techniques of Psychic Self-Defence Murry Hope (The Aquarian Press, 1983).
Practical Egyptian Magic Murry Hope (The Aquarian Press, 1984).
Larousse Encyclopedia of Mythology (Paul Hamlyn, 1959).
The Astrology of Personality Dane Rudhyar (Doubleday Paperback, Garden City, New York, 1970).
Fragments of a Faith Forgotten G.R.S. Mead (John M. Watkins, 1931 Third Edition).
The Mysteries of Eleusis Goblet D'Alviella (The Aquarian Press, 1981).
The Greek Myths, Vols. I & II Robert Graves (Penguin Books, 1955).
The Egyptian Mysteries Iamblichos (Wm. Rider & Son, 1911).
Thrice Greatest Hermes G.R.S. Mead (Theosophical Publishing Company, 1906).
A Dictionary of Symbols C.E. Cirlot (Routledge & Kegan Paul, 1963).
Memories, Dreams and Reflections C.G. Jung (Routledge & Kegan Paul, 1963).
Webster's Collegiate Dictionary (G. Bell & Sons, Ltd, London; G & C Merriam Co. Springfield, Mass. 1947).
Collins Music Encyclopedia (William Collins & Son, Ltd, 1959).

INDEX